SECRETS TO
Saving Big
ON COLLEGE

GILLIAN STUBBLEFIELD, M.A.

KREOLISH
MEDIA

Copyright © 2023 Gillian Stubblefield

All rights reserved.
Published in the United States by Kreolish Media, LLC
Michigan, USA

No part of this publication may be reproduced, distributed, or transmitted in any form or by any means, including photocopying, recording, or other electronic or mechanical methods, without the prior written permission of the publisher, except in the case of brief quotations embodied in critical reviews and certain other noncommercial uses permitted by copyright law.

The information provided in this book is intended to be accurate and authoritative regarding the subject matter covered. The book is sold with the understanding that the writer and publisher are not engaged in offering financial, accounting, legal, or other professional advice. If financial, accounting, legal, or other expert assistance is needed, it is recommended to seek professional advice from qualified experts.

ISBN: 979-8-9896850-0-4
Ebook ISBN: 979-8-9896850-1-1

PRINTED IN THE UNITED STATES OF AMERICA

Cover and Interior Design: Elysia Clapin

First Edition December 2023

Publisher's Cataloging-in-Publication data

Names: Stubblefield, Gillian, author.
Title: Secrets to saving big on college : a parent's guide / Gillian Stubblefield, M.A.
Description: Includes bibliographical references. | Ann Arbor, MI: Kreolish Media, LLC, 2023.
Identifiers: ISBN: 979-8-9896850-0-4 (paperback) | 979-8-9896850-1-1 (ebook)
Subjects: LCSH Student aid--United States. | College students--United States--Finance, Personal. | BISAC STUDY AIDS / Financial Aid | STUDY AIDS / College Guide | STUDY AIDS / Scholarship & Loans | REFERENCE / Consumer Guides | REFERENCE / Personal & Practical Guides
Classification: LCC LB2337.4 .S88 2023 | DDC 379.3--dc23

Kreolish Media, LLC
2075 West Stadium Blvd, #1874
Ann Arbor, MI 48106

To my daughters, my inspiration.

CONTENTS

INTRODUCTION	1
PART 1: Student Debt and Mistakes to Avoid	7
Chapter 1: The Problem with Student Debt	9
Chapter 2: Ten Mistakes to Avoid When Paying for College	25
PART 2: Strategies to Attend College for Less or Zero Dollars	47
Chapter 3: Strategy #1: Become Wise—Understanding Financial Aid	51
Chapter 4: Strategy #2: Chase the Money—Scholarships	85
Chapter 5: Strategy #3: Chase the Money—Generous Colleges	105
Chapter 6: Strategy #4: Apply for Access	117
Chapter 7: Strategy #5: A Degree at Half Price—Collegiate High School	125
Chapter 8: Strategy #6: Start Out at a Two-Year College	139
Chapter 9: Strategy #7: Tuition-Free Programs and Colleges	147
Chapter 10: Strategy #8: Consider the Military	155
CONCLUSION	171
REFERENCES	175

Introduction

It's the fall of your teen's last school year, and boom! You're in the college admissions process. You get news about colleges that are picky about who they let in and the cost of college, which can be very expensive. You start to feel nervous and wonder: "Will my kid get accepted? Do they have OK grades? How on earth can we afford this?" You have a million worries running through your head.

My daughters went through the process, and while their father and I had saved for college from the time they were in elementary school, the savings were still not enough to cover all their college costs—tuition, housing, food, fees, and so forth. Although my daughters had completed two years' worth of college credits (and an associate degree) by the time they graduated from high school, the cost of two more years of college for one daughter and slightly more than two for the other to get bachelor's degrees still required above and beyond what we had saved. In fact, one of my daughters chose a college that is now ranked as one of the most expensive colleges in the United States—Southern Methodist University.

In my experience as a college advisor, I've found one of the things that worries parents the most is college costs. Well, that's right after (or on par with) worrying about whether their child will get into college. While applying to college is very stressful, figuring out the financial aspect takes the cake. For one, it's not very transparent: few understand it, and it differs from college to college even in how the financial aid offers are presented. Add to this confusing mix is the practice of some colleges to consider a family's financial resources when making admissions decisions.

Figuring out how to pay for college goes beyond the first year. Each year your child is in school, the application process is repeated. In some cases, you might have to fill out the Free Application for Federal Student Aid (FAFSA) and the CSS Profile again. Listen, I've been there too. It's not fun.

If you commit to understanding the basics of financial aid, develop a plan to save for college, learn how to get your hands on free money, and consider some of the options outlined in this book to get a college education for free or at a reduced price, you will be well on your way to reducing the student debt burden for your child and/or yourself.

To develop a strategy to pay less for college, you must become financially savvy, learning everything you can about how to find the money to pay for college and how to get it. In my experience, the families who were able to get the most money for college started planning early—long before their child's senior year of high school. This is not to say that you are doomed if you did not start years ago. However, if you can start before high school or senior year, you'll have more options. This is obviously impossible for many families as they struggle monthly to make ends meet. If you were unable to save or start planning for college early, you can still take many steps to reduce college costs.

Several tools can help you estimate your college costs (e.g., net price calculators). You will find some straightforward steps to help you develop a clear and realistic plan to pay for college. Consider these before your student stares at acceptance letters as a senior. Most people begin to think about retirement long before they get there. Similarly, I encourage you to develop a plan early to cover college costs.

It's also important to have a conversation with your child about how much you can realistically contribute toward college expenses. If you haven't, though, don't panic; you have options too. This book will provide an overview of the financial aid process, how to maximize your chances of getting a good package, and some pro strategies to significantly reduce college costs.

There are billions of dollars available to students who want to attend college. Money is available in the form of scholarships, grants, and loans. Most students will pay for college with a mix of their own funds, scholarships, grants, and loans.

Helping families recognize the dangers of student debt has become a passion of mine. I still remember taking a financial aid class while completing my college counseling certificate. My instructor, through data, laid out a compelling case against student debt and implored us to keep our students from going down a path of financial destruction, which he defined as too much student debt. He encouraged us to do what we can by "crying, kicking, and screaming to keep families from going down this path to fulfill a dream college idea for a child." He jokingly stated that he would like to live in Maui on the beach but can't afford it.

That instructor encouraged me to help families think carefully about how much debt they take on to pay for college and examine the motives behind choosing a specific college. When choosing a school, families will make choices they believe are best for them. I'm just here to share some ideas that might keep you from taking on too much debt.

After you read this book, you will be empowered in the financial aid process and know that you have options to pay for college.

A FEW NOTES ON HOW TO USE THIS BOOK

Paying for college can impact both parents and the student, and the process can be confusing. This book assumes that you, the parent, are helping your child determine how to pay for college and taking an active role in the entire financial process. I do not assume that you will be paying for all college costs yourself. This should be a collaborative effort between the parent and student.

I have included many links to outside resources in this book as well as references to expert sources. In the interest of keeping this as simple as possible for you, I have listed and hyperlinked all references in the back of the book with specific note numbers for deeper research.

PART 1:
Student Debt and Mistakes to Avoid

CHAPTER 1: The Problem with Student Debt

Student debt is like carrying a heavy backpack full of bricks—it'll slow you down and make it harder to reach your destination!

Student debt in the United States is at an all-time high. As families struggle to cope with exorbitant college expenses, the average student loan debt continues to climb, according to *U.S. News & World Report*.[1] With approximately 43 million borrowers now burdened by nearly $1.75 trillion in student loan debt,[2] we must address this crisis. This book aims to provide effective strategies for reducing costs, so you and your student don't become part of this alarming statistic.

The best-case scenario for anyone preparing for college is getting a full-ride scholarship and avoiding student debt altogether. However, this might not be the reality for your family. Even with the most gifted student and the no-cost and low-cost strategies outlined in this book, you might still need to consider loans. This is why it's important to learn about student loans and their potential downside to help you make more informed decisions for your future and your child's future. If you must borrow, do it responsibly. Explore federal loans that usually have lower interest rates and compare them to private ones. Besides interest rates, there are other factors to consider when borrowing.

Student loans can help your child achieve a degree they might not otherwise be able to afford. And, according to research, a college education will pay off. A recent report from Georgetown University Center on Education and the Workforce found that "bachelor's degree holders earn 31 percent more than those with an associate degree and 84 percent more than those with just a high school diploma."[3] Still, you don't have to mortgage your house for your student to get a good college education.

First, you and your child should take time to research different colleges and the costs of attendance. In the United States alone there are nearly 4,000 colleges and universities, and the costs vary from a few hundred dollars to tens of thousands of dollars per semester. Colleges are categorized as public, private, two-year, four-year, research, and so on. Some are highly selective (think Ivies), some are moderately selective (meaning they accept about half of all applicants), and others accept most of the students who apply. Most two-year community colleges have an open admission or open enrollment policy; they accept most applicants who have a high school diploma or equivalent. You must determine what type of college is best for your child (socially, emotionally, and academically) and what you can afford.

Second, you need to understand the basics of financial aid and student loans. This includes understanding your costs (using a net price calculator; see Chapter 2) and the different types of financial aid available (grants, scholarships, and loans).

If you think you or your student will need to borrow, you'll want to research the different types of student loans available, the interest rates associated with each type, and the time it will take to repay them (using a loan calculator). You should also be mindful of the repercussions students face if they fail to repay a loan. This includes a possible decrease in their credit score and wage garnishment. Knowing these risks can help students decide whether taking out a loan is the right choice and how much to borrow.

It is important to understand the potential long-term effects of taking out too many student loans. These loans can be a significant financial burden for many years. It could also affect your ability as a parent to save for retirement.

STUDENT DEBT FOR THE NEW COLLEGE GRADUATE

Student debt is a significant issue for many new graduates, as higher education costs have steadily increased in recent years. The burden of student debt can significantly impact the financial health of new graduates, limiting their ability to purchase a home, start a business, or save for retirement. I will explain the impact of student debt on recent graduates and provide some strategies to reduce this debt in this chapter and later in the book.

New graduates with a large amount of debt can find their loans hard to pay off with what they earn from their first job. This debt can impact their financial health since they often have to spend a large percentage of their income on student loan payments, leaving them with less money to cover other expenses or save for the future.

So, what's a family to do? Colleges aren't reducing their prices. As a matter of fact, college price increases outpace inflation every year, and salaries are not keeping pace with inflation. According to the Education Data Initiative, the average cost of attending a public university in the 2022–2023 academic year was $25,707, while the average as an out-of-state student was $44,014. A private institution for that same period cost $54,501.[4] The cost of attendance at a two-year in-state college was $15,862 (tuition alone is $3,862).[4]

CHAPTER 1: The Problem with Student Debt

THE STATE OF STUDENT DEBT—A CRISIS?

Over and over on the news, we hear about a student debt crisis and trillions of dollars owed by current and former students—graduates and dropouts alike. But what does it mean for the individual?

According to the Urban Institute, "70 percent of students who receive a bachelor's degree each year have education debt by the time they graduate." The average student will graduate with a little over $30,000 in debt.[5]

Families starting the college admission process enter what I like to call a vortex. They all have one thing in common—they want the best for their child—but soon get caught up with emotions beyond their control. This can sometimes lead parents to take on more student debt than planned.

Additionally, many parents start out with little or no knowledge of the current state of college admissions, financial aid, and how they will pay for their child's education.

As a result, many families give into one of the dominant emotions in college admissions—fear. Fear that their student will not get in, fear that they will not get enough financial aid to afford college, and fear that if their student does not attend one of the top fifty colleges in the country they will be doomed to couch surfing—forever.

If you are unaware of what emotions are driving your decisions around college choice, you and your student could choose an unaffordable college.

Listen, I've been there. When my daughters were accepted to college, I wanted them to choose Vanderbilt. It didn't matter how much it cost. It was part sentimentalism, part fear, sprinkled with a bit of keeping up with the Joneses. I had fallen prey to the annual *U.S. News & World Report* ranking.

REASONS FOR THE STUDENT DEBT CRISIS

There are several reasons for the rise of student debt, but two of the main reasons are connected to the rising costs of tuition and books and lack of financial literacy.

RISE IN TUITION AND ROOM AND BOARD

According to the College Board, tuition and fees at public four-year institutions rose by an average of 2.6 percent for in-state students and 3.2 percent for out-of-state students between the 2019–2020 and 2020–2021 academic years.[6] Private college costs have seen a similar increase over this same period. In some cases, the tuition at public universities has increased more than private colleges due, in part, to reduced funding at the state level. To cover the increased costs, students are forced to take out larger loans for their education. Additionally, the costs of room and board have also increased.

COST OF BOOKS

The costs of college textbooks have also risen significantly in recent years, with the average student spending between $628 and $1,471 annually on textbooks, according to the Education Data Initiative.[7] The statistics of the hardship created by these increases are sobering: "25 percent of students reported they worked extra hours to pay for their books and materials; *11 percent* skipped meals in order to afford books and course materials."[7]

SYSTEMIC INEQUITY

Systemic inequity in our country has also contributed to the student debt crisis.

First, students of color are more likely to take out loans and have higher loan balances than white students. This is because students of color are more likely than white students to come from families of lower-income backgrounds and have less access to resources to pay for college.

Second, students of color are more likely to default on their loans since they often lack access to the resources necessary to make their loan payments. According to *Forbes*, "Black graduates are almost twice as likely to be unemployed as their white peers a year after leaving college.

And Black students are significantly more likely to find themselves in part-time or unpaid work after graduation."[8]

LACK OF FINANCIAL LITERACY

Lack of financial literacy can also cause students to make poor financial decisions. Understanding finances will help them budget, save money, and make sound decisions about how many loans to take out while in college. Having a thorough understanding of financial matters and being able to make informed decisions about money is what comprises financial literacy. According to an AIG-sponsored study, "47 percent of college students surveyed said they did not feel prepared to manage their money."[9]

This lack of financial literacy affects college students in several ways. For example, many are unaware of the details of their student loans such as interest rates and repayment options. Without this basic knowledge, students can easily fall into a cycle of debt and take out loans with unfavorable terms, which can lead to an inability to pay back the debt. Additionally, students may not be aware of other sources of funding such as scholarships, grants, or work-study programs. Lack of financial literacy can thus lead to a greater need for student loans and an increase in the amount of debt taken on.

Loans are not bad altogether. However, students need to have the financial savviness to determine how much is too much. Loans are often a necessary means to an end. To buy most big-ticket items, such as a home or car, most people will need to take out loans to fund part of those purchases. However, whenever borrowing—whether through a credit card or loans—you and your student need to do so responsibly; understanding the terms and how much you and they are likely to pay back after they graduate.

One of the best gifts you can give your child is to help them become financially savvy. By signing them up for a budgeting class and finding opportunities to discuss finances, you'll set them up for success beyond college. You can also commit to learning everything you can about financial aid—what it is, how to get it, and what your responsibilities are. It can feel overwhelming at first, but little by little, week by week, you'll begin to understand the terms. Don't give up and leave your financial aid outcome to fate.

Some places to get free financial literacy training are available through the Council for Economic Education at econedlink.org. This organization offers financial education for students from kindergarten through high school. The lessons are designed for teachers and students, with different versions based on type of use. You can access the classes directly or talk to your child's teacher or school district about adding them to the curriculum. The Internet-based lessons are designed to be delivered in a variety of formats and classroom settings.

WHY BORROW LESS?

If your child graduates with too much debt, they could be confronted with negative consequences. Some experts believe that students should not borrow more than the amount they expect to earn in the first year after graduation. Here is what your child could face with too much student loan debt.

1. HIGHER OVERALL DEBT BURDEN

When your child borrows more, they may graduate with a higher debt burden. With more debt, your child will have a higher debt-to-income ratio. This ratio is significant for creditors and landlords when deciding whether to lend money or rent to your student. With a higher debt burden, they may need a cosigner to buy a car or rent an apartment. If you can help them, that's great. But sometimes you may not qualify to be their cosigner.

2. MORE STRESS

Debt is stressful, especially student debt. Your child may worry about repaying their loans as they accumulate over the years. Subsidized federal student loans do not accrue interest, but unsubsidized loans do. If your child does not pay the interest on their unsubsidized loans as soon as they receive them, the interest will compound and increase their debt significantly by graduation. That's very stressful!

3. FEWER CAREER OPTIONS

Choosing to borrow more will likely mean your child must take the first job that comes along to pay off their loans. This may not be their dream job; they may have to put aside their career aspirations for now. More student debt means less financial flexibility.

4. LESS SAVINGS

Your child may not have any money left to save at the end of each month if they have too many student loans to repay. The first few years after college can be the most challenging financially, even without student loans. There are already so many bills—cell phone, Internet, groceries, car insurance, and entertainment, to name a few. Adding high student loan repayments to an already long list of expenses could keep your child from starting an emergency savings fund, saving for a down payment on a house, and even funding retirement.

5. LESS DISPOSABLE INCOME

Too much debt can postpone your child from enjoying their life after already spending four to six years earning their degree. With less college debt, they can live and enjoy some leisure and fun activities without worrying too much about money. They can dine out occasionally with friends and even travel.

6. RISK OF FINANCIAL CRISIS FROM DEFAULT AND DEFERMENT

Keep in mind that if your child defaults on their loan, they could end up with a host of other problems. The federal government can garnish their wages and even their Social Security. They will also never be able to get rid of a student loan by declaring bankruptcy. A student loan literally follows them to their grave. If they default on their loan or owe too much in student loans (or other loans/credit cards), it affects their credit score. A lower credit score translates to higher interest rates when they borrow money to purchase a car or buy a house. Depending on how much student loan debt they have, they might even need a cosigner to afford a loan.

Deferment can also place them in a precarious financial situation. If they have unsubsidized loans, every time they defer, they are still accruing interest that begins to compound. When students use deferment as an option, it could end up making the total interest they pay balloon significantly, even to as much as or more than the principal (the original amount they borrowed).

Student loans are a reality for most college students, and they will likely need to take out loans to pay for college. However, if they want to have greater financial and career flexibility, reduce their stress levels, and have a life after college, they must avoid too many student loans. In my experience, few people regret taking on too little debt.

CHAPTER 1: The Problem with Student Debt

BURDEN OF STUDENT DEBT ON STUDENTS WHO DROP OUT

Some of the students who bear the biggest brunt of large student loans are the forgotten students—those who start college but don't finish. They often leave with one or more student loans. Almost 40 percent of students who enter college as freshmen never complete college. According to the *Chronicle of Higher Education*, more than 75 percent of students have thought about leaving college due to mental health challenges.[10] Students who drop out without a degree find themselves in a worse position than if they had never gone to college. They now have loans that must be repaid but will have a hard time getting jobs reserved for college graduates.

Many students who drop out do so because they can no longer afford to pay for college or manage their living expenses. They may see their parents struggle to pay for the costs of college or worry about the whole idea of racking up so much debt before they even earn their first decent paycheck. This can lead them to focus more on work, which then can lead to them dropping out.

In addition to money woes, students arrive on college campuses stressed—they are away from their loved ones and support circle, they are not sure if they made the right college choice, and so forth. They are exiting one of the most stressful events in their lives—the college admissions process.

When students arrive stressed on campus, adding a burgeoning debt to the mix is a recipe for a crisis that could lead to students dropping out.

No one starts college to drop out, but this is the reality of higher education. These students tend to default on their loans at a higher rate than other students. Most employers do not reward you for *almost* completing a degree. In the corporate world, either you have a degree, or you don't. Often, the jobs for someone who drops out of college will not pay as well (Zuckerberg and Gates are two very few exceptions). So now with reduced opportunities for high-paying jobs, they still must pay back their loans.

In the next few chapters, I'll share five key things you and your child will need to do to avoid student debt pitfalls. In later chapters, I'll share practical strategies to reduce costs.

KEY TAKEAWAYS

Student debt is a problem for the collective population and the individual in the United States. To ensure you and your child do not end up taking on too much debt, there are three things you can do:
1. Understand all you can about financial aid (see Chapter 3).
2. Consider some no-cost or low-cost options to attend college through college access programs and the military or reduced-cost options through early college high schools (I will detail these options throughout the book).
3. Have a conversation with your child to discuss the reality of your financial situation, make a list that includes some affordable colleges, and discuss the options available to pay for their education.

CHAPTER 2: Ten Mistakes to Avoid When Paying for College

The pressure on parents to impress their friends is so great that sometimes they are willing to pay any college tuition and even sign their own economic death sentence!

The idea of graduating college with fewer student loans seems like an oxymoron. How do you graduate with less debt when the cost of a bachelor's degree can be as much as the cost of a house in some states? As a parent of two college graduates, I'm here to tell you it's possible.

I've had personal experience with some of these strategies. When we moved to Texas, my daughters were on track to attend a traditional high school for eleventh and twelfth grade. We flew out to Texas in the spring of their high school sophomore year to visit a few different high schools. We hadn't settled on a specific community to live in, so school choice was still up for debate. While we were visiting one of the high schools, we discovered that the students were taking classes for college credit through a nearby community college. When we dug further, we found the college also had a collegiate high school on its campus. The promise of finishing two years of college while in high school was like a siren song to my daughters. They loved the idea that accelerated their college journey, and I liked the idea of paying less.

My daughters graduated from high school with associate degrees and two years later, earned bachelor's degrees, saving us 50 percent of the total cost of college. They had a great high school education and were accepted into a range of colleges—from small to large and including some that were highly selective. The collegiate high school they attended was not perfect—it was a new program—but all in all, that experience set them up for success in college and beyond.

As you consider what strategies (listed in later chapters) to use to reduce how much you pay for college, here are ten mistakes to avoid when paying for college.

MISTAKE #1: FAILING TO APPLY FOR FINANCIAL AID

Failing to apply for financial aid is a mistake parents should avoid because it can significantly impact their family's financial security. When parents fail to apply for financial aid, they miss out on the potential to receive grants, scholarships, and loans to help them pay for college. Without this assistance, parents are more likely to take out high-interest loans to cover the cost of college, which can put them in a difficult financial situation.

There are many reasons families do not apply for aid. Some believe they make too much money and will be ineligible, others might think the process is too complicated, and yet others might need more information about the application. Whatever your reason, I'm here to tell you it is worth applying because you never know what you're eligible to receive until you do. And while you can use a net price calculator and a Free Application for Federal Student Aid (FAFSA) estimator to project your costs, it's just an estimate. A college could have received a large gift from a donor and might be able to offer more generous financial aid when your student applies to college.

There are a few reasons parents should apply for financial aid even if they think they will not qualify. First, the application process is relatively simple and can be completed online. Congress has taken steps to simplify the FAFSA. Completing the FAFSA is the first step in receiving financial aid. Sometimes, you will also need to complete the CSS Profile if your student is applying to a private college. Keep in mind that many colleges will only provide institutional scholarships and grants (free money from the college) to students who submit the FAFSA, CSS Profile, or other institutional scholarship application. Parents and students should review each college's website to find out if they have a separate scholarship application. You don't want to miss out on institutional funds!

The second reason why parents should apply for financial aid even if they think they will not qualify is that many colleges and universities offer institutional aid that is not based on financial need. It is essential to remember that applying for financial aid is not just limited to need-based scholarships and grants; many colleges also have merit-based scholarships and grants that require applicants to submit a financial aid application. Even if parents feel they may not qualify for a need-based award, their student may still be eligible for a merit-based award.

Therefore, parents should still take the time to complete a financial aid application as it could lead to additional funding.

Finally, applying for financial aid is important because it can help you save money in the long run. Don't count yourself out too early. Your student should apply even if they think they are not eligible for need-based aid or find the forms confusing; there are several places to get help. Every year around college application season, different groups offer free workshops to help families complete the FAFSA. Your student can also talk to their high school counselor for additional resources.

MISTAKE #2: NOT SAVING FOR COLLEGE

Investing in your child's education early can help them avoid taking on large student loan debts and give them more flexibility when it comes to choosing a college. Saving for college early can be a great way to ensure your child's success and give them the best opportunities for the future.

Two key benefits to saving for college are avoiding debt and increasing flexibility. Families can avoid taking out large loans to cover tuition by saving for college early. This can make a world of difference, as student loan debt can be crippling.

Furthermore, by saving for college, families can have more flexibility regarding the type of college they choose, as they won't be limited by financial constraints.

If you are unable to save for college, all is not lost. Other ways exist to cover college costs. You and your student will be able to apply for financial aid when they apply for college.

You and your student could also begin looking for gift aid (money you don't have to pay back) before they even apply for college. In some cases, students can begin applying for scholarships as early as ninth grade. Think about how much money you and your student can bank if they apply for a few scholarships every semester before senior year. If they target the right scholarship and submit a top-notch application, they could end up with a nice scholarship chest by the time they are ready for college.

However, it is always a good idea if you can cut back on spending in some areas to save for college. Families can save for college through Roth IRAs and 529 plans. You can research these further online and talk to a financial advisor to learn more about the pros and cons of these instruments.

AN OVERVIEW OF 529 PLANS

A 529 plan is a tax-advantaged investment vehicle designed specifically for educational purposes. There are two types of 529 plans: prepaid tuition plans and savings plans, each offering unique benefits to help families save for college expenses. Explore the differences between these options and how they can be used effectively in your college savings strategy.

Prepaid Tuition Plans: What Are They?

Prepaid tuition plans allow you to purchase units or credits at participating colleges and universities at current prices, locking in the cost of future education today. These plans typically cover tuition and mandatory fees. Still, they may not include room and board costs, or other living expenses associated with attending college.

Prepaid plans are:
- Ideal for those who have a specific in-state school in mind for their child's postsecondary education.
- Protected against inflation—the value of the plan increases along with rising tuition rates.
- Limited in flexibility, as they only cover eligible institutions within that particular state-sponsored program.

529 Savings Plans: What Are They?

A 529 savings plan allows more flexibility when choosing an institution since funds can be used toward any eligible college or university, including some international schools. A 529 savings plan can pay for more things than just tuition and fees, like room and board, books, and supplies. It also allows for more versatility with investment options that have the potential for higher returns if the market does well.

529 savings plans are:
- More versatile investment options with the

potential for higher returns based on market performance.
- Flexible—funds can be used at any eligible institution regardless of state affiliation.
- Riskier than prepaid tuition plans due to exposure to market fluctuations that may affect future income available for your child's education.

Weigh the advantages and disadvantages of each 529 plan to determine which best fits your family's needs. Consider factors like the likelihood of attending an in-state versus out-of-state school or a private institution when evaluating prepaid tuition plans. For those seeking more flexibility or who are uncertain about their child's college destination, a 529 savings plan may be the wiser choice.

FIVE TIPS TO GET INTO THE HABIT OF SAVING FOR COLLEGE

1. Set a goal. Target how much you want to save for college. Make sure the goal is realistic and achievable. Consider setting up a 529 plan or other college savings account to help you reach your goal.
2. Track your spending. Monitor your spending habits so you know exactly how much money you are spending each month. This will help you to better understand how much you can save for college.
3. Set aside money every month. Make it a habit to set aside a certain amount of money each month to save for college. This will help you stay on track with your goal of saving for college.
4. Take advantage of tax benefits. Look into the tax benefits for college savings accounts. Many states offer tax credits or deductions for college savings.
5. Automate savings. Program your savings plan so you can set it and forget it. This will ensure that you are putting money away each month without having to think about it.

In summary, saving for college can have a significant impact on reducing student debt by lowering the amount of money borrowed. Saving for college can help families allocate funds to cover the costs of tuition, textbooks, room and board, transportation, and other college expenses.

MISTAKE #3: NOT PLANNING FOR COLLEGE EARLY

It is never too early to begin planning for your child's college education.

Some of the most common mistakes parents make when paying for college are not planning early and not preparing their student to compete for merit aid at top colleges or for other scholarships.

When you begin planning early, you will be able to ensure that your student is building a competitive profile. Not only will you have time to ensure they are taking all the courses required to graduate but also that they are enrolling in honor and Advanced Placement (AP) courses and engaging in extracurricular activities to build a strong résumé that most competitive colleges expect.

Additionally, you will be able to build a college list early and ensure your student is taking the classes required for admission into those colleges. For example, I worked with a student who wanted to apply to a public university in California. However, he did not realize until it was too late that he needed to have one course from visual and performing arts. Had he known this before senior year, he would have taken it during the summer. Sadly, he had to pass up on the opportunity to apply to a dream school of his. It's important to check what a college requires for admission before your student's senior year in high school. This way, you can see if your student has what the college wants; if not, they'll have enough time to meet the requirements before applying.

While you should not stress your kids out about college in ninth grade, you can begin mapping out a plan for extracurricular activities, which is an important component of a college application.

Planning early gives students time to thoughtfully select extracurricular activities—ones they are truly passionate about and not just activities that will win merit aid. Extracurricular activities can benefit students beyond making them competitive for scholarships. It is a great way for them to explore areas of interest or pursue a sport they like. They can also learn about teamwork, strengthen their leadership abilities, and build strong time-management skills that they will need in college.

In the end, a strong academic and extracurricular profile can translate to merit aid and admissions into colleges offering generous financial aid.

MISTAKE #4: OVERLOOKING SCHOLARSHIP OPPORTUNITIES

Applying for local and national private scholarships is an important way to reduce the overall cost of college. With the rising cost of college tuition, scholarships can provide much-needed assistance.

Organizations, businesses, and foundations often offer private scholarships dedicated to supporting students in their educational and career pursuits. These scholarships can provide funds to help pay for tuition, books, and other college expenses. For example, your student can apply for local scholarships available through Rotary International, your church, or other community organizations or national ones like the Coca-Cola or Dell scholarship.

While the high-dollar scholarships tend to be national, the local ones should not be overlooked. Those tend to be less competitive. Local private scholarships are available in almost every city and state and can often provide a significant amount of money for college. They are often awarded to students who demonstrate financial need, academic excellence, and/or community involvement. In most cases, only students from that area (city/state) can apply.

Private scholarships can allow students to focus on their studies without the burden of accumulating debt.

To learn more about finding scholarships, refer to Chapter 4.

MISTAKE #5: THINKING FRESHMAN SCHOLARSHIPS WILL BE OFFERED THE NEXT YEAR

Parents should avoid the mistake of thinking that the scholarship their student receives as a freshman will be available for the other years of college, because scholarships are usually awarded on a year-by-year basis. You might be excited to receive a very generous financial aid package from your child's dream college, but before you do your happy dance, find out whether you can expect a similar package each year if there are no major changes in your family's income. Ask whether any scholarships received are renewable or if they are one and done.

Some scholarships are only awarded to freshman students and unavailable in future years. Some scholarships will require that students continually demonstrate that they are meeting certain criteria (e.g., a certain GPA or course load) to remain eligible for the scholarship. Additionally, the scholarship funding may vary from year to year, meaning that even if a student is eligible for the same scholarship, the amount of money they receive may differ.

For these reasons, parents must be aware that the scholarship amount awarded each year could look very different.

MISTAKE #6: NOT UNDERSTANDING THE FINANCIAL AID PROCESS

Figuring out financial aid for college can be very confusing. However, understanding the process is important for parents to make sure they are getting the best value for their child's college education.

At the very least, commit to learning the sources of financial aid, how and when to apply, the types of aid you will qualify for, college cost comparisons, and an estimate of your potential out-of-pocket costs. It is also important to build a college list that includes schools that offer generous need-based aid or merit aid depending on your financial circumstances and the college's policy. Many highly selective colleges will not offer merit aid but offer very generous need-based aid.

For example, to access most federal, state, and institutional financial aid, you and your child will need to apply using the FAFSA, which becomes available in October each year. Some aid is also available on a first-come, first-served basis and might have different deadlines. The more you know, the more funds you might be able to access to pay for college.

Navigating the financial aid process does not have to be overwhelming. By understanding the process, researching the different types of financial aid, completing the FAFSA, and setting a budget, parents can save money and make sure they are getting the best deal on their child's college education.

For more information about how financial aid works, please see Chapter 3.

MISTAKE #7: GETTING CAUGHT UP IN COLLEGE RANKINGS

Parents sometimes rely heavily on college rankings and want to provide their child with the best possible education, according to the gospel of the college rankings in *U.S. News & World Report*. And there is absolutely nothing wrong with that, but can you afford it? And is a college ranked at thirty-two worth more than the college ranked at forty-five? Is it going to be rated that way next year? In the last year, many colleges have started to rebel against the rankings for different reasons, some more self-serving than others.

College rankings have played a role in turning college admissions into a zero-sum game. The more selective college admissions have become, the more parents feel they must do and pay whatever it takes to give their child a leg up on the competition. Some families become so enamored with the few dozen brand-name colleges the media loves to promote that they may take on an unreasonable amount of student debt.

Many parents also feel a sense of pride in having their child attend a prestigious college and may be willing to go into debt to make that happen.

U.S. News & World Report and *Princeton Review* rankings are a good way to begin researching colleges. However, while the top fifty colleges may offer some distinct advantages (name recognition by employers, access to professional networks, etc.), there are dozens of other colleges that also provide students with a top-notch education and access to great job opportunities.

Parents should instead focus on a variety of factors, such as the college's academic reputation, cost of attendance, and student life, as well as whether the college is even a good fit for their student.

In an article published by Payscale.com, Dr. Bridget Terry Long acknowledges that "debt is a reality of higher education today, and some debt is fine if it makes possible a beneficial educational investment. However, the level of student debt that is reasonable depends greatly on the school attended and major."[11] For example, taking out $75,000 in student loans could be a good investment for an engineering major but not so much for an art major who might earn far less in their career. Some experts believe students should not borrow more than they expect to earn in their first year after college.

Don't be so eager to chase after a brand-name college that you lose perspective of the cost and overestimate the value of the education. Colleges that might not make the *U.S. News & World Report* top-fifty list can offer your student a top-notch education and student experience at a great value. For example, you can find colleges that are committed to supporting and graduating their students with $30,000 or less in student debt through the Coalition Application. Each of the 150 member colleges have a six-year graduation rate of at least 60 percent of their students.

There are also some amazing colleges that are under a coalition called Colleges That Change Lives. This coalition was established based on the premise of a book written by a retired *New York Times* education editor and journalist. He set out to change the college admissions rat race and create a more student-centric process that focuses on what's best for the student with the belief that great colleges exist beyond the Ivies.

As a parent, you owe it to yourself and your student to find a college where your child will thrive academically and socially instead of a college everyone is talking about. It is also vital to keep cost in mind.

While it is important to provide your children with the best possible education, you must also consider the long-term implications of taking on too much debt. Try to strive for balance. With a little research and some careful planning, you can make the best decisions for your family's financial future.

MISTAKE #8: NOT HAVING A FRANK DISCUSSION ABOUT COLLEGE CHOICE AND FINANCES

The road to graduating with fewer student loans begins with communication between parents and children well before college. It's almost as important as "the talk" we give our kids when they become teenagers. Parents should discuss with their child, preferably before high school, how they plan to cover college costs and how much they can afford to contribute.

Most parents, even those who have saved for college, are unable to cover 100 percent of college costs. Having this talk is important to helping your child determine, long before senior year, how they can position themselves for scholarships to reduce college costs. This might also affect the types of schools your student decides to target. If money is an issue, you may want to target very generous colleges.

Having a frank and open discussion up front is better than waiting for your child to fall in love with a school, apply, get accepted, and then discuss the budget reality. If you are only willing to fund a certain amount each year, tell them that now. I have known parents who have told their children that they are only willing to pay the costs of an in-state tuition, so if they want to go to a more expensive college, it's on them. These parents have given their student the opportunity to work harder on academics or pursue private scholarships over the years.

Waiting until senior year to discuss how and who will pay could spell trouble. You should not, however, rule out going to college altogether because you think you can't afford it.

MISTAKE #9: NOT APPLYING TO COLLEGES THAT HAVE A HIGH STICKER PRICE

I know it sounds counterintuitive to what I've been talking about in looking for the best college at the lowest price (best value). However, since most students will not pay sticker (or advertised) price, don't just look at the price listed online and dismiss a college.

Instead, use the tools available to get an estimate of your costs. One such tool is a net price calculator that will provide an estimate of what you might expect to pay after scholarships and grants are considered (see how to use a net price calculator in Chapter 3).

Another such tool is the Federal Student Aid Estimator. This tool will give you an estimate of any federal aid you are likely to receive based on your family's financial profile.

One of the best tools to find colleges with generous financial aid is collegedata.com. You can search colleges based on the amount of financial need they offer and learn the percentage of students receiving merit aid. By clicking on the "Financials, Debt & Aid" tab, you can adjust these to find colleges that meet up to 100 percent of your family's need. Your financial need is determined by a calculation using the FAFSA and CSS Profile, used by some private colleges (see Chapter 3 for more information).

MISTAKE #10: GIVING INTO PEER PRESSURE

Yes, adults can give into peer pressure too.

For many parents, the goal of sending their children to prestigious institutions feels like an obligation, not an option. This pressure can come from peers, family, and the culture of high expectations that many communities demand.

It can be overwhelming to provide children with an education that is at the same level or better than those around you. Hearing how few students Stanford or Harvard accepts creates a great deal of stress in parents, and they think their child will not get into any college. So, when their teen receives their first acceptance letter from a prestigious college, even one without generous financial aid, a parent might feel relief and then may get in over their head to pay for it.

While getting your child into the best college possible is not a bad idea in and of itself, it should not come at the cost of your family's financial stability. As a rule and as mentioned before, most experts believe that a student (or parent) should not borrow more than the student expects to earn in their first job after graduating from college. For example, if your child is planning to become a marketing specialist, which had an average annual income of $55,000 in 2023, you should aim to keep the total amount you borrow under $55,000.

CHAPTER 2: Ten Mistakes to Avoid When Paying for College

Another thing to keep in mind is that almost half of students do not finish college. I know what you are saying: your child will not be that one, and I hope they're not. No one believes their child won't graduate from college. Yet year after year, I've met families whose children faced academic dismissal. I hope that in the future, the number of students who do not finish college will be negligible. However, the truth is students arrive on campus with a great deal of stress, and they drop out for many reasons, including things related to their health, family, academics, or something else. Life happens.

The last thing you want to do is encourage your child to go deep into debt and then not have a degree in the end. A Department of Education analysis conducted in 2022 and cited by the White House revealed a staggering reality—"nearly one-third of borrowers have debt but no degree."[12] In many cases, students who have not completed their degree earn less than if they had a degree, and some default on their loans when the interest adds up over time.

A parent's quest to get their child into the "perfect college" can also affect how much they save for their own retirement. As the cost of a college education continues to rise at a faster rate than salaries, many parents must choose between paying for their children's education and providing for their own retirement.

It is important to remember that every family's financial situation is different. As a parent, you should consider alternative ways to pay for college such as scholarships, grants, and other strategies outlined in this book.

Ultimately, it is important to make the decision that is best for your family, regardless of what your peers are doing or saying. After all, it's your money and your life.

PART 2:

Strategies to attend college for less or for zero dollars

HOW TO USE THIS SECTION

Now that you understand the student debt crisis and see why you should avoid it, I will lay out eight strategies to attend college for free or for significantly less than the sticker price.

Finding ways to pay for college can be daunting. With tuition costs rising, many students and their families are left feeling overwhelmed and unsure of how they will be able to cover the enormous costs associated with college.

Saving for college is an important way to reduce your costs, and Chapter 2 provides a short primer on 529s. However, please note it is for informative purposes only and should not be deemed professional investment advice. Please consult your financial advisor for personal investment strategies.

However, if you haven't saved anything, there is hope. In this book, we explore many different strategies to pay less for college, from understanding financial aid and applying to generous colleges to joining college access programs and military academies. We'll also discuss winning scholarships, ROTC, and other options for reducing college costs. So let's dive in and explore the different ways you can pay less for college.

I've laid out eight strategies, so feel free to use the ones that make the most sense for your family. You might be able to combine some of the following options to arrive at zero student debt. Good luck!

CHAPTER 3:
Strategy #1: Become Wise—Understanding Financial Aid

―――――――――

Start early and plan smarter. Being financially savvy can help you make informed decisions about college and save you lots of money!

Financial aid is an important tool in helping students pay for college and graduate school. Understanding the different types of financial aid available and the process of applying for aid can make the difference between graduating debt-free or facing a mountain of debt. Financial aid can come from the federal government, state government, colleges and universities, private organizations and businesses, or individuals.

Grants and scholarships are the most common forms of financial aid, and these awards do not typically have to be repaid. Grants and scholarships can help to cover tuition, fees, and living expenses. Loans are also available and must be repaid upon graduation.

It is important to understand one of the first steps to access financial aid—the FAFSA. To access federal aid, you will need to complete the FAFSA. Keep in mind, many private colleges also require students to fill out the CSS Profile. The CSS Profile (or the College Scholarship Service Profile) is an online application used by more than eight hundred colleges and universities to determine a student's eligibility for nonfederal financial aid.

Both the FAFSA and CSS Profile gather information about your family's financial situation and help colleges determine your eligibility for aid. After completing the FAFSA, the college or university may provide you with an award letter outlining the types and amounts of aid you will receive.

THE LEARNING CURVE

When my former spouse and I embarked on the college admissions process with our daughters, we naively thought we had a handle on how much it would cost us at the colleges our daughters were likely to consider. I remember thinking that with the college savings we had been stashing away since the girls were in elementary school, we could do this. Since ninth grade, we had started building college visits into our road trips. The campus visits intensified once

CHAPTER 3: Strategy #1: Become Wise—Understanding Financial Aid

they were in eleventh grade. The sweltering summers in Texas did not slow us down.

The planning that went into these trips was extensive. The days leading up to the road trips would mean sending my daughters links to read to prepare for the visit and forms to use to take notes while we visited the campus. One Saturday morning, just around sunrise, we set out for a short road trip. It was a local visit to Southern Methodist University.

We filled up on breakfast, then headed out on the tollway, free of rush-hour traffic, for the less than thirty-minute drive to the campus. With the fresh morning breeze seeping in through barely cracked windows, we entered wide tree-lined boulevards that hid brick buildings that looked like they had decades of stories to tell. They were framed by well-manicured lawns and small patches of bright annuals, strategically placed to impress. I heard myself say "wow," and echoes of that exclamation from the back seat. All that was missing was piped orchestra music. We drove through the boulevards, found parking, and then began our trek to the admissions office. It wasn't long before we were greeted by eager student ambassadors. As we entered the room reserved for the presentation, we noticed a couple dozen parents and students nervously glancing around the room. Before long, the session started. "Welcome to SMU!" the admissions rep shouted. This was the start of our love affair with SMU.

However, I had spent so much time focused on the cost of attending each college my daughters had on their lists that I did not factor in other costs, such as the price of a second car since the kids were going to be attending different schools. We always thought they would attend the same college. And I did not factor in the cost of one daughter changing housing in the middle of a semester, which meant furnishing a new space.

Like many families, I discovered the full cost of college after my daughters had gone through the admissions process and fallen in love with their college choice. Families often face this stark reality after their student has fallen completely in love with a college, only to find out that (a) they didn't get as much in scholarships or grants as they expected, (b) the financial aid package contained more loans than they could conceivably pay back after a degree in, say, history, or (c) the college costs were significantly more than they originally thought.

What made the financial aid process confusing was that I didn't fully understand it. While I had started a tutoring business that offered test prep around the time my daughters were seeking out colleges, I did not specialize in helping students in college admissions. Financial aid was like a foreign language to me. I would later pursue and complete a certificate in college admissions from UCLA, which included a very comprehensive study of financial aid and a practicum that allowed me to advise students at a Dallas area private school. As we were going through the exercises in my financial aid class, that included a full analysis of the FAFSA and the calculations used, I quickly realized my knowledge had barely scratched the surface of financial aid.

I now want to share the information I've amassed from personal experience, formal education, and working in the field as a college advisor.

For families looking to reduce college costs, I would recommend understanding the financial aid process as a first step.

After you have a basic understanding of the process and what it is and is not, you will have more realistic expectations about how much you will pay for college. This will help you to develop strategies specific to your needs and financial situation and likely reduce your costs.

Understanding and applying for financial aid can make a huge difference in the cost of college. Taking the time to learn about available financial aid can help make college affordable and put your student on the path to graduating debt-free.

Let's jump right in to learning about college costs and what financial aid is and isn't.

THE COST OF COLLEGE

Take one look at the cost for college and you might think you were looking at a four-year plan to buy your first home. Add room and board, books, and other costs, and you might think you are about to take on the US national debt. The cost of attending college continues to rise at an alarming rate.

Add to this the highly competitive nature of getting into college these days and it is understandable why this is the most stressful time for families. According to researchers at EducationData.org, an organization that collects data and statistics about the US education system:

- The average cost of attendance for a student living on campus at a public four-year in-state institution [for 2023–24] is $26,027 per year or $104,108 over four years.
- Out-of-state students pay $27,091 per year or $108,364 over four years.
- Private, nonprofit university students pay $55,840 per year or $223,360 over four years.

The cost of college has increased more than individual earnings over the past decade. Between 2010/11 and 2020/21, public universities have seen a 45 percent increase in tuition compared to a 28 percent increase for private universities in that same period.[4]

College costs are made up of tuition, room and board, books, and other fees. When you hear the term "cost of attendance" (COA), this is what is included. Most students, however, do not pay the full COA, receiving discounts through scholarships and grants.

CHAPTER 3: Strategy #1: Become Wise—Understanding Financial Aid

Private colleges' COA can appear higher than public colleges. However, private colleges often give bigger discounts than you can expect from a public college or university. A recent survey by the National Association of College and University Business Officers found that in the 2022–2023 school year, private colleges gave first-year, full-time students an average 56.2 percent institutional discount, while all undergraduates received on average a 50.9 percent discount—both were record highs.[13] This means students received gift aid that covered more than half of their tuition.

Public universities do not generally engage in the same level of tuition discounting as private colleges. Due to less state funding, public universities have also had to raise their tuition at a higher rate than private colleges to cover their costs.

As a result, in some cases, your costs of attending a private college could be less than that of a public university. This is why it's important to know your true costs of attendance. You cannot rely on what your friend or cousin paid. Their financial situation and academic profile might be different from yours. Plus, colleges could have different institutional goals from year to year.

Your student should choose their college with cost in mind. However, it's hard to figure out how much you will pay by just looking at the sticker price. For an early estimate of your costs, use a net price calculator. For instructions on how to use one, refer to the section on net price calculator toward the end of this chapter.

WHAT IS FINANCIAL AID?

Financial aid is made up of free money (grants and scholarships) and loans to help you and your student pay for college. Other ways many families pay for college is by offsetting costs with their income and savings. Of course, not everyone can afford to save for college.

There are many sources of financial aid, including the college, federal government, or state government.

Outside or private scholarships are also available—the term "outside" refers to funding from outside the college. These scholarships are generally available through companies, such as a Coca-Cola scholarship; nonprofit organizations; private foundations, such as the Jack Kent Cooke Foundation or the Gates Foundation; local civic organizations, such as Rotary or Lions Club; and even churches.

Your first step to access financial aid is to submit the FAFSA, which becomes available in October each year.

For simplification, when I refer to "financial aid" in this chapter I'm not talking about private or outside scholarships. Those are addressed in Chapter 4. Instead, I'll talk about the scholarships available through colleges and the federal or state government.

NEED-BASED AID VERSUS MERIT AID

Financial aid often falls into two categories—need-based aid and merit aid. Need-based aid is reserved for students who demonstrate financial need. On the other hand, financial aid that is based on merit is reserved for students who demonstrate strong academics, athletics, or other special talents.

TYPES AND SOURCES OF AID (WHERE IT COMES FROM)

The main types of financial aid are grants, scholarships, and student loans. The largest source of financial aid is the federal government, followed by colleges.

- **Grants** are considered gift aid and do not have to be repaid. They can come from the federal government, state government, or the college itself.
- **Scholarships** are considered gift aid and do not have to be repaid. Your student can be awarded a scholarship based on their financial need or merit. Scholarships can be awarded by state governments, colleges, or private organizations.
- **Student loans** are considered self-help financial aid that must be repaid. Loans are available through the federal government, colleges, banks, and other private institutions. Here are the different types of federal loans available to undergraduate students and parents:

- **Subsidized loans** are available only for students who demonstrate financial need. The government pays the interest while your student is in college. Students must begin repaying the loan, with interest, after they graduate.
- **Unsubsidized loans** are available for all students. Students have the option to pay the interest while they are in college (the recommended option) or allow the interest to accrue (not recommended) and begin repaying the interest with principal (original amount borrowed) when they complete college.
- **Parent PLUS loans** are available to parents of undergraduate students who are still dependents.
- **Work-study** is considered self-help financial aid that is made available for your student to earn income through part-time work on campus, and, in some cases, off campus. Work-study jobs are not guaranteed; students must apply for these positions.

The federal aid available to families includes:
- Federal Supplemental Educational Opportunity Grant (students)
- Pell Grant (students)

- Stafford subsidized loan (students)
- Stafford unsubsidized loan (students)
- Parent PLUS loan (parents)
- Work-study (students)

Most students will end up with some mix of grants and/or loans available through the federal government, state government, or college directly. Some colleges offer loans. Many states offer specific grants to students, and in some cases, they are available to undocumented students.

GRANTS

For the 2023–2024 academic school year, the Federal Pell Grant maximum award was $7,395. The amount you receive will be based on your family's financial need and the Student Aid Index (SAI, formerly known as EFC, or expected family contribution). Generally, families with an income below $60,000 qualify for either a full or partial grant, while those earning under $20,000 usually receive the full Pell Grant. Other factors that affect the award amount include the cost of attendance (COA) and whether the student is attending college full time or part time.

The Federal Supplemental Educational Opportunity Grant is reserved for undergraduate students and awarded based on need and a first-come, first-served basis. Each college receives a certain amount of money from the federal government, and when that runs out, that's it.

STUDENT LOANS

More than half of all students attending college will take out a loan, according to the Urban Institute. As a result, the average student will have a debt exceeding $30,000 when they graduate.[14]

Student loans are considered financial aid, and most students' awards will contain some loans. The loans can be subsidized or unsubsidized, depending on your family's financial profile. No credit check is required, and all students are eligible for one or more loans.

Subsidized Loans

Subsidized loans are need-based, which means only those families earning below a certain income will receive them. The federal government will pay the interest on the loan while the student is in school, and students have six months after graduation or if they go on half-time status to begin repaying the loan. Loan terms can stretch from ten to thirty years, depending on how much you borrow.

Unsubsidized Loans

Unsubsidized loans are available to students with or without financial need. They differ from subsidized loans when it comes to who pays interest. With unsubsidized loans, the student is responsible for the interest as soon as the loan is awarded. A good rule is to begin paying the interest while in school; otherwise, your student will soon discover the nightmare of compound interest.

Parent PLUS Loans

Parent PLUS loans are available for parents and graduate students. Parents cannot have poor credit (bankruptcy, excessively late payments, etc.) or they will not qualify. If a parent does not qualify for a Parent PLUS loan, students can get an increased amount of unsubsidized loans.

Private Loans

Private loans are available through banks and other private institutions, including colleges. Because of the high rate of interest, these should be a last resort. Repayment terms on these loans are generally not favorable and they tend to have variable interest rates. Variable rates mean the rates could fluctuate over time. While these loans might be easy to come by, the interest could end up costing you and your student a lot.

HOW TO APPLY FOR FINANCIAL AID

To apply for financial aid, you and your student will need to complete the FAFSA, available through studentaid.gov/fafsa. It is used by colleges to determine your eligibility for federal grants and loans, state grants and scholarships, and the college's own scholarships and grants. The FAFSA is your first step toward accessing financial aid to cover your student's college costs, and it becomes available on October 1 each year.

Most students are eligible for some kind of financial aid, so even if you think you make too much money, applying makes sense. Your student must be a US citizen or eligible legal resident with a Social Security number to qualify for federal financial aid. Additionally, certain states, such as Texas, provide financial aid to undocumented students who qualify as state residents. The kind of aid your student receives is based on your financial need—your family's financial need is based on income and assets.

WHO IS RESPONSIBLE FOR FILLING OUT THE FAFSA?

The FAFSA is technically the student's responsibility. However, you are most likely to initiate this process as a parent. No matter who starts it, it must be a *joint effort* since it requires information from you and your student. In most cases, the bulk of the financial information (e.g., income and assets) will be from you. The same information is required from students, but teens often do not have any earnings or assets to include.

All students applying for financial aid using the FAFSA will be classified as independent or dependent. How students are classified will determine whether parental information must be included in the application.

DEPENDENT STUDENTS

A student under twenty-four years old is considered a dependent if they are not married or do not have legal dependents. A dependent student needs parental information to complete the FAFSA.

In some cases, a dependent student might be unable to get financial information from their parents. In those cases, they can still complete and submit the FAFSA; however, they will have to contact the financial aid office at the college they plan to attend.

INDEPENDENT STUDENTS

A student twenty-four years and older, married, and/or with legal dependents is considered an independent student for purposes of the FAFSA. They can apply for financial aid without any information from their parents.

In some cases, students under twenty-four might be considered independent and, therefore, do not need their parents' information. For example, students who are married, have dependents, were in foster care, are pursuing a master's degree, or are homeless are considered independent in terms of the FAFSA. There are some other exceptions as well. To learn about all of them, please visit studentaid.gov and type "dependency status" in the search bar.

Plan to complete the FAFSA around the time your student applies for college; you will be able to use the

FAFSA application to apply for financial aid. Parents and students will complete different parts of the application. Here are some of the things you will need:

1. FSA ID (you'll have to create one; learn how: https://studentaid.gov/h/apply-for-aid/fafsa)
2. Social Security number
3. Driver's license (if applicable)
4. Federal income tax returns—both for parents and the student (if applicable)
5. Records of untaxed income (if applicable)
6. Records of assets
7. Alien Registration Card (if applicable)
8. List of colleges under consideration

FAFSA CHANGES IN 2024–2025 SCHOOL YEAR

A new version of the FAFSA will be released by the US Department of Education in December 2024. The changes stem from the 2020 FAFSA Simplification Act that Congress passed to make the FAFSA easier for families to complete.

According to the Brookings Institute in a recent report, some of the changes will mean:

- lowering or losing the discount for families with more than one child enrolled in college
- Increasing the number of families eligible for Pell (due to change in income criteria)
- Raising the student/parent income exemption when figuring out financial need, and

- Reducing the amount families with low incomes are expected to pay.[15]

The new FAFSA will also replace the term/formula "EFC" with a new term/formula: Student Aid Index (SAI). The updated FAFSA will also have fewer questions.

FINANCIAL AID DEADLINES

You and your student should be aware of three deadlines when completing the FAFSA: the federal deadline, the state deadline, and the college deadline.

The FAFSA becomes available on October 1 annually and allows you to apply for financial aid almost a year ahead of the academic year in which your student plans to attend college. Although the federal deadline to submit the FAFSA is approximately twenty months after it becomes available, you will need to meet most colleges' and states' deadlines much sooner. In addition, some financial aid funds are available on a first-come, first-served basis, so submitting the FAFSA soon after it is available in October has its advantages.

Here are the three deadlines you and your student should be aware of:
- **College deadline.** Each college has its own financial aid deadline, and it is generally the first of the three deadlines. Some colleges will have a priority deadline and a regular deadline. Priority deadlines allow you to access the most funds

for college, so plan to submit the FAFSA and any other required applications as early as possible. To find the deadline for a specific college, you should check on the college's financial aid website.

- **State deadline.** Many states offer financial aid and have different deadlines for eligibility for state funds. To find out more about any state's program and deadline and what, if any, aid you might qualify for, please visit the National Association of Financial Aid Administrators' website (https://www.nasfaa.org/State_Financial_Aid_Programs).
- **Federal deadline.** If you are applying for federal funds, the FAFSA can be filed approximately one year before you begin college, beginning on October 1. The deadline is about twenty months later. For example, if you planned to attend college in the 2024–2025 academic school year, the FAFSA was made available on October 1, 2023, with a deadline of June 30, 2025 (the end of the academic year). However, you should be aware that some federal funds are limited and are awarded on a first-come, first-served basis, so the earlier you file, the greater your chances of receiving an award. In addition, the FAFSA you submit will, in many cases, be used for federal, state, and institutional funds, so following the earliest financial aid deadline would be prudent.

You are required to list at least one college (with a maximum of twenty) to receive the FAFSA Submission Summary (FSS) generated upon filing the FAFSA. In the past, the FAFSA limited students to ten colleges, although they were able to add other colleges after they submitted the FAFSA.

In addition to the FAFSA, most private colleges will also require that you complete the CSS Profile.

The FAFSA will allow you to access federal aid, while the CSS Profile allows you to access the financial aid from the college's own funds.

WHAT HAPPENS AFTER YOU APPLY?

After completing the FAFSA, you will receive a FAFSA Submission Summary (FSS). The report will provide an estimate of Pell Grant or student loans the student is eligible to receive. It will also state the amount of money parents and the student are expected to contribute to the student's education. This figure is called the Student Aid Index (SAI)—formerly known as expected family contribution (EFC).

The SAI number is generated by a formula that takes the parents' income and assets and the student's income and assets into consideration.

Families usually will pay more than the SAI since most colleges do what's known as gapping. This basically means they do not give you all the financial aid you technically qualify to receive. For example, if the full cost of attending a college is $48,500 and your SAI is $12,500, your financial need is technically $36,000. However, it doesn't mean your student will automatically receive financial aid of $36,000 from the college. Most colleges will only be able to offer you part of that amount, which would be considered gapping. Gapping in financial aid award happens when the amount of financial aid offered by a college or university is less than the amount of money needed to cover the total cost of attending.

Also keep in mind, all financial aid will not come in the form of grants and scholarships (gift aid). In most cases, part of your student's financial aid package will include loans. There are only a small number of colleges that give loan-free financial aid packages and meet 100 percent of financial aid.

While most of the need-based federal financial aid is reserved for low-to-moderate income families, your student may qualify for need-based aid from some private colleges even if your family is classified as high income.

Some private colleges, especially the highly selective ones, are known for their generous need-based aid even for high-income earners. For example, at Rice University, families earning between $75,000–$140,000 are eligible for aid to cover full tuition, and those earning between $140,000–$200,000 will receive aid to meet half of their tuition.

AFTER YOU SUBMIT THE FAFSA; WHAT NOW?

After you submit the FAFSA, a FAFSA Submission Summary (FSS) will be emailed to you within a few days (sometimes it can take a few weeks). You can also access your FSS at Federal Student Aid (https://studentaid.gov/) by logging in and using the FSA ID you created when you filled out the FAFSA. The report summarizes everything you listed on your FAFSA and will also be sent to the college(s) listed on your FAFSA.

The FSS will list your family's SAI and your student's eligibility for federal financial aid. Colleges use the SAI listed on your FSS as a basis for making financial aid awards.

Once you receive your FSS, check it for any errors. If you find an error, you may be able to make changes to your FAFSA. Check with Federal Student Aid for more information on what you can and cannot change.

Each college your student listed on the FAFSA will receive a report called the Institutional Student Information Record. If admitted to those colleges, your student will receive a financial aid package with their award. The award can be made up of scholarships, grants, and loans. And if they are really lucky, a full-ride scholarship.

FINANCIAL AID AWARD

If your student is accepted to one of the colleges that received their FSS, the college will prepare a financial aid award letter that outlines the COA and all of the scholarships, grants, loans, and/or work-study your student has been awarded. The letter may also contain your SAI. The financial aid administrator at their college will be your best source of information regarding when and how your financial aid award will be paid.

HOW TO APPEAL YOUR FINANCIAL AID AWARD

Your student was accepted into their dream school, but you did not get the big financial aid award you were expecting. Now what? Well, do not despair. If your circumstances have changed since you submitted your financial aid application, submit a financial aid appeal to the financial aid office at the school in question.

What Is a Financial Aid Appeal?

A financial aid appeal is a process available to college applicants to request additional funds or a better financial aid package than the one that was offered.

Most, if not all, colleges will have procedures in place to help you file an appeal. To get started, visit the college's financial aid website or reach out to the college's office of financial aid.

What Is a Good Reason to Appeal a Financial Aid Award?
A major change to your family's income or unusual medical expenses are good reasons to appeal. However, these are not the only reasons.

Financial aid administrators get to use "professional discretion" or "professional judgment" in considering special and unusual circumstances. In other words, if you give them the reason and the proof to offer you more money, they can—provided the college has the funds.

Remember, it's not enough to say you are unhappy with the award—most people are—and expect an instant increase in your award. Before they can show you the money, you have to show them the proof. Here are some good reasons to appeal a financial aid award:

- Loss of income due to layoff or termination.
- Unusually high medical bills due to illness or hospitalization of a family member.
- Unexpected life event—the death of a parent or immediate family member.
- An estrangement between the student and their parents.
- A natural disaster experienced by the student and parents.
- A correction to income/assets on the FAFSA, CSS Profile, or other financial aid application.
- A better financial aid award from another college.

HOW DO I SUBMIT A FINANCIAL AID APPEAL?

Most colleges have a process for appealing a financial aid award. To ensure you are submitting the right documents, check with the college's website or financial aid officer on the requirements.

Cornell University, for example, has specific forms you have to submit when making a financial aid appeal. Some other colleges might only require a letter with supporting documents. Even if a college has forms to complete, attaching a letter with a substantive and heartfelt appeal, if permitted, could do the trick.

The following are five tips to for you and your student to appeal their financial aid award.

1. Document Special Circumstances

Prepare a letter or email (based on the financial aid office's directions) respectfully requesting additional funds and documenting your changed circumstances. If a parent either lost a job, became ill, got a divorce, or took on the responsibility of supporting an elderly family member, add that to your request. You will also need to include copies of any documentation you have—termination letter, medical bills, and so forth. Providing supporting documents will help you build a stronger case and make it easier for the financial aid officer to use professional judgment in your favor.

2. Leverage Other Offers

Did you know you can use higher financial aid offers from other colleges to bolster your financial aid appeal?

For example, if you received a higher financial aid offer from another college your college considers a peer (or competitor for the same students), it might match it. If your child is in the top 10–25 percent or even top 50 percent of applicants in terms of academics and/or have a special talent, you might have more leverage. Many colleges want to boast about the academic prowess of their students in *U.S. News & World Report*. The lower your child falls in the applicant pool, the less leverage you might have.

Regardless, express gratitude for the offer of admissions and the financial aid package. If the college is your child's top choice, say it. However, it is equally important to stress that an increase in the college's gift aid—scholarships or grants (money you don't have to pay back)—would make it possible to attend.

3. List Any New Merit Awards or Academic Improvement

Additionally, when writing your appeal, your student should mention any new awards they have received since submitting the application. If they have received an academic, leadership, athletic, or other award, make sure to mention it. Doing so might make your student a much more attractive candidate if they weren't so already.

Remember, colleges are very interested in your child's achievements because if they look good, the college looks good.

4. File the Appeal in a Timely Manner

If possible, don't wait until it's close to college decision day (May 1) to appeal your financial aid. Colleges will take this to mean that they are part of your back-up plan.

Of course, if circumstances change close to decision day, you will have no choice but to submit the appeal at that time. Keep in mind that funds are often limited, and other students will be appealing their financial aid award too.

5. Follow Up

If you haven't heard back from the college in a week's time, you may want to follow up with the financial aid office by phone or email. If your student's appeal is denied, ask if you could submit any additional documents to bolster your appeal. If the answer is still no, then you have two choices for your student: (1) attend and find a responsible way to cover the cost or (2) go to a more affordable school.

Whatever you do, don't forget to send the financial aid officer a thank-you letter even if you did not win your appeal or get the big increase in grants and scholarships you were expecting.

Taking the time to submit a well-thought-out financial aid appeal with supporting documents will increase your chances of getting more money.

Keep in mind, if you are lucky enough to win your financial aid appeal, the same amount of money might not be offered every year you are in college. The devil is always in the details.

Ask the financial aid administrator how much of your financial aid package is renewable for your student's sophomore, junior, and senior years. You should also ask about what criteria they have to meet. Read the fine print, and good luck on your appeal!

BONUS: HOW TO KNOW YOUR COSTS BEFORE YOU APPLY

USING THE FEDERAL STUDENT ESTIMATOR

If you want to learn your federal financial aid eligibility before you apply, there is a tool available called Federal Student Estimator (https://studentaid.gov/aid-estimator/). This tool from the US Department of Education can help you estimate your eligibility.

To use it, you'll need to provide basic information, such as the number of people in your family and your income. The tool will then give you an estimate of the types of aid you may qualify for, such as Pell Grants, federal work-study, and direct subsidized and unsubsidized loans.

To get started, go to the Federal Student Estimator website and click "Start Estimate". You'll create an account then be taken to a page where you can enter your personal information, family size, and income. After you've filled out the form, click "Next" to see your estimated aid eligibility.

USING A NET PRICE CALCULATOR

To find out what aid you might be eligible to receive before you file the FAFSA, use the net price calculator found on each college's website.

A net price calculator can be an excellent tool for understanding the true cost of attending college. It can help you estimate the amount you'll need to pay for tuition, fees, room and board, and other expenses. To use a net price calculator, you'll first need to input basic information such as your family's income and the number of people in your family. The calculator will then use this information to calculate an estimated cost of attendance.

Depending on the calculator, you may be able to enter more detailed information, such as expected scholarship awards, state and federal grants, and other financial aid awards; some may ask for your SAT/ACT score and GPA. Once you've entered all the information, the calculator will use it to generate a net price estimate reflecting the total cost of attendance minus any financial aid awards you're eligible for.

In the end though, the only way to truly know how much financial aid you will receive is to submit the FAFSA and, whenever required, the CSS Profile.

──────── *Where to Find a Net Price Calculator* ────────

- Net price calculators are available on most college's websites. All Title IV institutions that enroll full-time students pursuing a degree or certificate are required to have one. To find it

for an institution, visit this website and type in the name of the college: https://collegecost.ed.gov/net-price
- There is also a net price calculator on the College Board's website: https://professionals.collegeboard.org/higher-ed/financial-aid/netprice/participating-schools.

USING A STUDENT LOAN CALCULATOR

The aim of this book is to help your student earn their education for free or almost free. This means some of the strategies listed might not cover 100 percent of college costs. However, the strategies aim to minimize the use of loans.

If you and/or your student end up needing to take out loans, you must understand your options before you do so. The best way to do that is by using a student loan calculator to compare different loan terms and better understand their potential costs.

A student loan calculator can estimate how much you need to borrow to cover your tuition and other expenses. It can also help you determine an affordable repayment plan and decide which loan best fits your situation. The best part is that student loan calculators are readily available online.

Here are three reasons to use a student loan calculator before you borrow:
1. **Estimate your payments:** A student loan calculator can help you and your student

determine how much they will be expected to pay each month after graduation. This way, you can plan ahead and make sure you are comfortable with the payment amount before you borrow the loan.
2. **Compare different loans:** Different loans will have different repayment terms and interest rates. A student loan calculator can provide a side-by-side comparison of different loans, helping you and your student make an informed decision about which one is best for you and them.
3. **Calculate the total cost:** Student loan calculators can also help you to calculate the total cost of the loan, including interest, over the course of the loan.

You can find student loan calculators online, typically on websites of student loan lenders or other finance websites like Bankrate.

HOW TO FIND THE AVERAGE FINANCIAL AID COLLEGE AWARDS

There are tools available to help you determine if some colleges are a good financial fit. You can see the academic profile (average GPA, test scores, class rank) and the average financial aid students received at a particular college.

Collegescorecard.ed.gov shows the average financial aid a student can receive by providing a breakdown of

CHAPTER 3: Strategy #1: Become Wise—Understanding Financial Aid

the average amount of financial aid awarded to students at a particular college. This includes grants, scholarships, loans, and work-study. You can compare the average financial aid awarded to students at different colleges to get an idea of what kind of aid you can expect to receive if your student chooses to attend a certain school. You can also see the median total debt after graduation.

Here's how to access this information:
1. Go to collegescorecard.ed.gov and type in the name of the school you would like to compare in the search bar.
2. Click on the schools you would like to compare and scroll down to the "Cost" tab.
3. Click "Compare Schools" to see a side-by-side comparison of the average annual cost of the two schools.

The cost comparison will show the average net price and the annual cost of attendance. The average net price is the average amount a student pays after accounting for scholarships and grants. The average annual cost of attendance includes tuition, fees, books, supplies, housing, and other expenses. You can see what students pay based on their family income when you scroll down to the "By Family Income" category.

Use the cost comparison to help you decide which school will be the most affordable based on your financial circumstances.

KEY TAKEAWAYS

If you don't have time to read all the chapters in this book, you should at least read this one. The foundation of making good financial decisions is understanding financial aid and the options available to pay for college. To help you plan, it's also important to get an estimate of your costs before your student applies to college.

Here are four things you should do to estimate your costs:
1. Use a net price calculator.
2. Use the federal student aid estimator.
3. Find the average aid by income using collegescorecard.com.
4. Use student loan calculators to learn what your loan payments might look like based on how much you borrow.

FINANCIAL AID RESOURCES

NET PRICE CALCULATORS
- Search "name of college" + "net price calculator" on a web browser.
- College Board's net price calculator: https://professionals.collegeboard.org/higher-ed/financial-aid/netprice/participating-schools.

STUDENT LOAN CALCULATORS
- Student loan calculator—Sallie Mae: https://www.salliemae.com/college-planning/tools/student-loan-repayment-calculator/

FEDERAL STUDENT AID ESTIMATOR
- https://studentaid.gov/aid-estimator/

CHAPTER 4:
Strategy #2: Chase the Money—Scholarships

Winning a scholarship is like taking a big step toward success—you just have to believe you can do it.

Another way to fund a college education and keep from amassing high student debt is by applying for and winning scholarships. There are millions of dollars of scholarships available for the taking. Although this chapter is focused on private scholarships—those available outside of a college—you should also pay close attention to the ones available through your student's college. If you want to reduce your overall student debt, your student should apply for both types of scholarships.

Private scholarships are funds given by individuals, businesses, or organizations, for example the Gates Foundation or your local Rotary club, to support students in their educational pursuits, such as tuition, books, or living expenses. These scholarships range in size from a few hundred dollars to a full ride and can be based on academic performance or other terms set by the donor.

Winning a big scholarship could net you enough money to pay for the full costs of college. For example, receiving a private scholarship like the Gates Scholarship could be a major blessing for anyone looking to attend college without debt. This last-dollar scholarship (covering gaps between federal and state grants/scholarships and tuition) is given to outstanding minority students who demonstrate exceptional academic achievement and leadership. The scholarship covers the full cost of attendance, including tuition, room and board, and other related expenses not covered by your financial aid and your family's expected contribution, based on the Free Application for Federal Student Aid (FAFSA).

This means that students who are awarded the scholarship, in most cases, can attend college without having to take out loans or worry about affording the costs of school. In addition to providing students with financial relief, the Gates Scholarship also has the potential to open up new opportunities. Many scholarship winners are given access to exclusive internships, research opportunities, and other professional development experiences that can give them a leg up in the job market. By taking advantage of these prospects, students gain valuable work experience and build their résumés to help them stand out from the competition after graduation. With the Gates Scholarship, many students can attend college without loans and set themselves up for long-term success.

To maximize your chances of winning a scholarship, your student needs a game plan. As the saying goes, "Before anything else, preparation is key to success" (Alexander Graham Bell).

When you hear about students winning scholarships, you often think they are top of their class or in some other way outstanding. The truth often looks very different than that.

Yes, when you have stellar academics it's easier to compete for some scholarships, but there are thousands of scholarships available to the student who is in the academic middle. There is practically a scholarship available for students from every walk of life—based on leadership, major, ethnicity, locality, interests, financial need, organization affiliation, and the list goes on.

Don't shy away from applying for some of the big ones if you feel they are a good fit. Some of the biggest scholarships in the country are from the Gates Foundation, Coca-Cola, and the Jack Kent Cooke Foundation.

While serving as a college advisor in Texas, I worked with a student who applied for a very competitive and generous scholarship—the Terry Scholarship. The Terry Scholarship offers up to a full-ride scholarship to high school seniors entering one of eleven universities in Texas, including Texas A&M University, the University of Texas at Austin, and the University of Texas at Dallas. He had to prepare for the interview round but was not confident that he would get past that round because he was talented in the creative arts. To him, only the top students in their class, the class president, or those who excelled in math and science would receive it.

Despite his uncertainty about winning this scholarship, I worked with him over a couple of days in a mock interview to help build his confidence and prepare him. I helped him tell his story, share his strength, and accept the outcome. He had the interview and nailed it. He was so appreciative of my help in preparing him for that interview. The truth is, I saw in him what he had a hard time seeing: I knew he had an excellent chance of winning.

About a year later, I was at the university he was attending, and I heard someone say, "Hello, Mrs. Stubblefield." I turned around and saw the young man with an enormous smile. He couldn't stop thanking me for helping him get to the university he wanted to attend. And, more importantly, winning the scholarship to pay for it.

My encouragement to your student is not to count themselves out before they even try. They should apply for competitive scholarships if they meet the criteria and can commit to preparing a solid application.

While going after the big scholarships may lead to a large payoff, I want to encourage your student to chase the small, local ones too. Your student has a higher chance of winning local scholarships. Yes, some are smaller than the top national ones, but they will add up.

TYPES OF SCHOLARSHIPS AVAILABLE

Scholarships can be an excellent way to fund your college education. They come in a variety of types, including local, state, national, hobby, demographic, major and interest, need-based, academic, and athletic. They all can help you pay for tuition and other related expenses. Each of these types of scholarships come with unique criteria and requirements, so it is important to research the different types of scholarships to find the best fit for you.

LOCAL

As the name implies, local scholarships are those available from local civic groups, organizations, and churches. They are generally only available to students from specific local school districts, cities, counties, or zip codes.

An advantage of local scholarships is a smaller applicant pool (which means less competition).

There are all types of local scholarships. Some stand alone and others offer wraparound support services.

STATE

Students who are residents of a given state may be eligible for state scholarships—e.g., Michigan Achievement

Scholarship, Georgia HOPE Scholarship, and Tennessee HOPE Scholarship. Such scholarships come with their own set of qualifications that must be met, with state residency being one of them. Certain scholarships are merit-based and take into account a student's high school GPA and standardized test scores. Other awards are based on need, paying attention to a student's financial situation and capacity to fund their education.

NATIONAL

If your student has done well in their studies and has been an all-round top performer, there is a good chance that they could get a national scholarship. National scholarships are more competitive than local or state ones, so if your child has been an honors student and acted as a leader in their community, they might have a good shot at getting one. Showcasing commitment to and involvement in their community is a great way to boost their chances of success in their application.

Some national scholarships like the Dell Scholars Program target high schoolers from underserved populations, requiring a GPA of 2.4 or higher. So, even if your child is not a top student in school, don't discount their chances. Check out this list of top-dollar scholarships (https://thecollegepod.com/7-of-the-biggest-scholarships-you-can-win/) to begin a search.

HOBBY

Did you know there is free money out there just for doing what your student loves to do? Whether they're into playing an instrument, singing, gaming, writing, art/doodling, knitting, crocheting, or anything else, there could be a scholarship just for them! The best part is, all they have to do is show how passionate they are about their hobby, and they might be rewarded with free money for pursuing their interests. What could be better than that?

For example, they can enter the Doodle for Google (htttps://doodles.google.com/d4g/prizes/) contest if they are a serious doodler or artist and win up to a $30,000 college scholarship and $50,000 tech package for their school or nonprofit. Plus, Google will display their artwork on Google.com (yes, *that* Google.com!) for 24 hours.

DEMOGRAPHIC

There are many scholarships available for students of different backgrounds and genders. For instance, the Ron Brown Scholar Program (https://ronbrown.org/apply/ron-brown-scholarship/) is open to African American students, providing them with a wonderful opportunity to pursue their educational dreams. Additionally, there are scholarships available for Hispanic/Latino, Asian Pacific American, and Native American students as well as those who are first-generation college-bound or from other underrepresented groups.

MAJOR AND INTEREST

Your student's college major could have an influence on the amount of scholarship money they can receive. If they are studying in fields such as healthcare, education, science, technology, engineering, or math, they may be eligible for specific grants or scholarships related to their major. Most scholarship search engines have a filter feature that allows you to search for scholarships by major, area of study, or something similar.

But even if they plan on majoring in something outside these areas, they can still find scholarship awards that do not require pursuing a particular major.

COMMUNITY SERVICE

Your child doesn't have to be a perfect student to qualify for a good scholarship. Many scholarships reward those who choose to volunteer and be active in their community. For example, the GE-Reagan Foundation Scholarship (https://www.reaganfoundation.org/education/scholarship-programs/ge-reagan-foundation-scholarship-program/) program awards students $10,000 to $40,000 per year to students who show they have made a positive impact in their community.

To be eligible, applicants have to "demonstrate the attributes of leadership, integrity, drive, and citizenship within their communities, schools, and workplaces" and maintain a 3.0 GPA, among other things. No matter your child's academic status, volunteering and making a difference in their community can make them eligible for some of these great rewards.

ATHLETIC

If your child is a student athlete and dreams of playing college sports at a Division I or Division II NCAA school, they might have a chance to get a scholarship. To be eligible, they need to meet certain requirements like having good grades, being skilled at their sport, and following the rules set by the NCAA. It's also important for them to show good sportsmanship and have a positive attitude, as that can increase their chances of receiving a scholarship.

Scholarship programs are a great way to recognize hard work and a commitment to excellence in sport and academics.

NEED-BASED

If your family earns below a certain income, your student will often qualify for need-based aid at most colleges. However, many private scholarships also offer need-based scholarships to families with low income and, in some cases, even middle income.

The income cutoff point will be different for each scholarship program. You may be asked to submit the FAFSA or some other type of income verification with your scholarship application.

ACADEMIC

An academic scholarship is awarded to a student who has demonstrated outstanding academic achievement.

These types of scholarships are often considered merit-based, meaning that they are given to students who have a proven track record of high grades and test scores, or other special talents.

SEVEN OF THE LARGEST SCHOLARSHIPS

Seven of the largest private scholarships in the United States provide a great opportunity for students to reduce their tuition costs and make college more affordable. These scholarships are funded by large corporations, foundations, and individuals to help deserving students pursue their educational goals. Some of these scholarships are achievement-based, need-based, or a combination of both.

Seven of the largest private scholarships include:

1. Jack Kent Cooke Foundation College Scholarship Program (https://www.jkcf.org/our-scholarships/college-scholarship-program/)—up to $55,000 per year
2. Gates Millennium Scholars Program (https://www.thegatesscholarship.org/scholarship)—full COA after financial aid
3. Coca-Cola Scholars Program (https://www.coca-colascholarsfoundation.org/apply/)—$20,000 scholarship
4. Cameron Impact Scholarship (https://www.bryancameroneducationfoundation.org/

scholarship#eligibility)—four-year, full-tuition scholarship
5. Davidson Fellows Scholarship (https://www.davidsongifted.org/gifted-programs/fellows-scholarship/)—$10,000, $20,000, or $50,000
6. Dell Scholars Program (https://www.dellscholars.org/scholarship/)—$20,000 (plus a laptop and textbook credits)
7. Ron Brown Scholar Program (https://ronbrown.org/apply/applicants/)—$40,000 ($10,000 per year)
8. Burger King Scholars Program (https://www.burgerkingfoundation.org/programs/burger-king-sm-scholars)—$1,000 to $50,000
9. Horatio Alger—$10,000 to $25,000

This list does not include all of the high-dollar private scholarships available. To find more, search one of the scholarship search engines such as The College Pod (https://thecollegepod.com/).

Some other big scholarships are available through college access programs (see Chapter 6 on college access programs). Two of the biggest programs are Posse and QuestBridge.

WHERE TO FIND SCHOLARSHIPS

Now that you know what types of scholarships are floating around out there, you're probably wondering how to get your hands on them. These resources will lead you straight to them.

- **Scholarship search sites:** You can use online search databases, like The College Pod (thecollegepod.com) or Scholly (myscholly.com), to narrow searches based on your student's background, achievements, and interests. You can also use an app like RaiseMe (raise.me), which allows students to start earning scholarships from colleges in the ninth grade. However, it is important to note that students can only use these scholarships at the college that awards them if they get accepted to the college.
- **High school counselors:** Your student can talk to their counselor at school as an easy way to find scholarships they're eligible for. The counselor may know about local scholarships and the scholarships past students have won to point your student in the right direction.
- **Local organizations:** Starting the search at the local level is a great place to begin. To find local scholarships, you can use a scholarship search database or easily do a Google search. Simply type in your city name with the words "scholarships" or "foundation scholarships" (e.g., "Dallas scholarships" or "Dallas Foundation scholarships") and you'll

find dozens of scholarships available. The local Rotary, companies, and foundations in your city and state often offer scholarships exclusive to county, city, or state residents. Work your way up from there, looking at state and national level opportunities. Remember, the bigger the applicant pool, the more competitive it will be.
- **State scholarships:** You can find grants and scholarships available through your state by visiting https://www.nasfaa.org/.

HOW TO CREATE A WINNING SCHOLARSHIP STRATEGY

START EARLY

Did you know that your student could start applying for college scholarships as early as ninth grade? However, scholarships will require a significant investment of time. Some will require essays, letters of recommendation (LORs), and maybe a copy of your child's transcript. If your student waits until it's close to the deadline to start, they may not be a strong applicant. Worse yet, they could end up missing the deadline.

GET ORGANIZED

Since each scholarship application will have different requirements, it might be helpful to create a spreadsheet. You and your student can list the name of the scholarship and the deadline and have separate columns to check whether it requires an essay or LOR. Create a column to add the link to the application and record the date when your student submits it.

Also, it's important to figure out how much time your student will need to set aside each week or month and commit to it. Encourage them to add the time to their calendar on their phone or the family's physical calendar—whatever makes it easy to remember.

Creating a spreadsheet will help you and your student keep track of everything.

KEEP TRACK OF THE DEADLINE

This one could have gone under the preceding paragraph, but I can't tell you how many times I've heard students say they missed out on applying for scholarships because they didn't even know the deadline for the application. Have your student put an alarm on their phone if they need a reminder—one that will alert them one week before the due date, not the day before. This way, they still have time to prepare a decent applicant package if they're a bit behind.

BUILD A STRONG LIST—IF YOUR STUDENT MEETS THE CRITERIA

As you and your student make a list of potential scholarships, you'll need to figure out if they meet each scholarship's criteria or if they come close. If so, it might be worth applying. If not, look for another one instead of wasting time. Now if the scholarship asks for a 3.5 GPA and they have a 3.49 and can tell a story to show why they think they are a good candidate, give it a shot. Maybe they have extenuating circumstances where perhaps they were unable to get a tutor because of finances. However, please be aware that some places use these criteria to whittle down an overwhelmingly large applicant pool, so this is where they might weed people out—anyone below a certain GPA.

FOLLOW THE RULES

If the organizations ask for two LORs, only submit what's required—not more or less. And, if they ask for an essay on a certain topic, don't have your student write what they think the organizations want to hear. I've served on several scholarship review boards, and if a student submitted an essay that had nothing to do with the topic we requested, I would think they were just trying to recycle an existing essay. Doing this will not win your student any points in a competitive scholarship landscape.

GET STRONG LORS

Have your student ask for LORs from their teachers, mentor, pastor, job supervisor, or someone who could speak to the strengths the application is trying to highlight. Make sure your student gives enough notice to their recommenders to ensure they can do a good job of capturing the things your student would like highlighted. Your student should provide them with a copy of their résumé and some information about the application. If your student wants them to highlight a specific project, task, or strength with an example, ask them to do so. Remember specific examples strengthen an LOR. If it's just all generalizations and vagueness, it's not as powerful and will not provide a strong support of your student's candidacy for the scholarship.

CREATE A RÉSUMÉ/ACTIVITY SHEET

Encourage your student to build one that showcases their academics, community, and leadership engagement. If they babysit younger sisters or brothers, include that and the hours spent doing it each day or week.

WRITE A STRONG ESSAY

Not every scholarship requires an essay, but if it does, go strong. There is nothing worse than reading an essay that sounds like the writer did not even try or wrote it an hour before submission. I have read essays from high school students with very bad grammar and, in a couple of cases, where there was no capitalization.

CHECK THE APPLICATION TWICE

Before your student hits "send," they should check to ensure their application is error-free. They shouldn't be in such a rush to send it off only to realize they not only made errors, but they did not attach the documents requested.

KEY TAKEAWAYS

With college costs rising faster than your income, it's a good idea to look for money wherever it's available. Many companies, foundations, and local groups offer scholarships. Some people rule themselves out even before trying, thinking their student can't compete. However, I have sat on several scholarship committees, and you would be surprised by how few applications some scholarship programs receive.

Here are some things to help you and your student develop a good scholarship strategy:

1. Stay organized. Create a scholarship tracker in Excel to stay on top of the moving parts of a scholarship application.
2. Start early. Beginning in ninth or tenth grade, your student should set aside a few hours a month to search and apply for scholarships. As it gets closer to senior year, your student will have to ramp up their efforts.
3. Search in the right spots. Use scholarship search engines such as thecollegepod.com and cappex.com to

find scholarships. Your student should also ask their high school counselor who will know where other high school students have won scholarships.
4. Have your student put together a strong application, write a thoughtful essay, keep up their GPA, and get involved. Encourage them to find ways to maintain or raise their GPA and get help if they encounter academic challenges. They should find opportunities to volunteer or get involved in an organization that will provide leadership opportunities. Their academic credentials and community engagement (they could start a business or nonprofit too) go a long way in making their applications more competitive.

CHAPTER 5:
Strategy #3: Chase the Money—Generous Colleges

---

*Don't be afraid to explore.
You never know what financial aid gems you
could uncover at an unknown college!*

If you are looking for a lot of help to take the bite out of your child's college costs, you should look for generous colleges, and somewhat generous colleges—they run the gamut. Colleges that meet 100 percent of financial need are in short supply. The irony of this is most of the very generous colleges (those meeting most of your financial need, often without loans) are generally some of the most competitive colleges.

Getting all or most of your financial need met will ensure that you pay the least amount of out-of-pocket costs. College can be a huge financial burden, so the assurance that your financial need will be fully met can be a huge relief. Just so you know, most colleges do not meet all of your financial need.

"So, what exactly is my financial need?" you wonder. Well, I'm glad you asked. Read on.

WHAT IS FINANCIAL NEED?

Your financial need is calculated using the cost of attendance, or COA (tuition, room and board, and fees) minus your Student Aid Index, or SAI (formerly known as expected family contribution, or EFC). Your family's SAI will be determined by the financial information you include in your FAFSA. The SAI can go as low as -$1,500, and it is the amount of money the government/college has determined your family can contribute towards your student's college costs.

Here is a simple calculation to demonstrate how your EFC/SAI is determined (university and calculation used below are for demonstration purposes only):

Cost of attendance @ University of Miami (2023–24)	$75,330
Student Aid Index (SAI)	$40,000
Your family's financial need is	**$35,330**

WHAT MAKES A COLLEGE'S FINANCIAL AID GENEROUS?

Colleges that meet most or all of your financial need are considered generous. A college that has "generous" financial aid covers a significant percentage of financial need—about 80 to 100 percent. In the example above, a generous college would provide scholarships and/or grants to cover the $35,330, or most of it. Colleges that have "not-so-generous" financial aid might do what is known as gapping—when they meet only part of your family's need. If the college above gaps your financial aid, they might only cover a portion of that $35,330 (your financial need). Keep in mind, most colleges do not meet full financial need, and many that do will provide loans to meet that need so it's yours to pay back.

Colleges run the gamut when it comes to what is considered generous financial aid. A few may meet your family's full financial need with or without loans. Many colleges will consider themselves meeting your full need with a financial aid award that includes both grants and loans. Colleges that do not count loans in this equation are by far the most sought after. Ironically, they are also the most competitive colleges.

However, there are only a handful of colleges that offer "no-loan" financial aid packages. Some "no-loan" colleges only extend this type of financial assistance to students from low-income backgrounds, while others extend it to students from middle- and higher-income backgrounds. There are also some state universities that only offer "no-loan" packages to students from that state. In most cases, the "no-loan" financial aid at the state level is reserved for students from low-income backgrounds.

NO-LOAN COLLEGES

Check out fourteen of the most generous colleges below. These colleges made the "Financial Aid Honor Roll" in Princeton's Review's 2023 edition. Some of them meet 100 percent of demonstrated need; a few without any loans.

These are the colleges that give the most financial aid (not factoring in loans). If your student has the academic chops to get into these colleges, then go for it. If they are lucky enough to get in, they could conceivably graduate with very low student debt or, perhaps, none at all.

"No-loan" private colleges:
1. Bowdoin (ME)
2. California Institute of Technology (CA)
3. Carleton College (MN)
4. Grinnell College (IA)
5. Haverford College (PA)
6. Kenyon College (OH)
7. Pomona College (CA)
8. Princeton University (NJ)
9. Vanderbilt University (TN)

10. Vassar College (NY)
11. Washington University in St. Louis (MO)
12. Williams College (MA)
13. Yale University (CT)

HOW TO FIND GENEROUS COLLEGES

To get an idea of which colleges have generous financial aid, you can use collegedata.com or the College Scorecard (https://collegescorecard.ed.gov/). Both tools will provide information on the average amount your family might receive based on your income range. Both platforms allow you to compare several colleges. This can help you figure out how much aid your student might receive if they are accepted into each college.

College Scorecard allows you to find the average cost a family paid at a specific school based on income. Each family's situation will be different, so you could pay more or less than the average.

To find the average annual cost a family with your income range is paying at a particular college, follow the steps below. This is only an estimate, but you can get a sense of how much gift aid—grant and scholarship money—that college might award.

1. Go to Scorecard.org.ed.gov.
2. Enter the college you are interested in.
3. Under the "Costs" tab, you can review the

average annual cost a family in your income bracket might pay for the college.
4. Compare up to ten colleges.

You can also find your personal net price on this website.
1. Go to Scorecard.org.ed.gov.
2. Enter the college you are interested in.
3. Under the "Costs" tab, select the "Net Price Calculator" (green button; see screenshot below), and you will be taken to the college's net price calculator.
4. Enter the required information, including student's grade, dependency status, parent income, and assets.
5. Click "Submit" when you're done.
6. Review the results on the next page.

The average estimated net price is the average cost a family will pay for college based on their income.

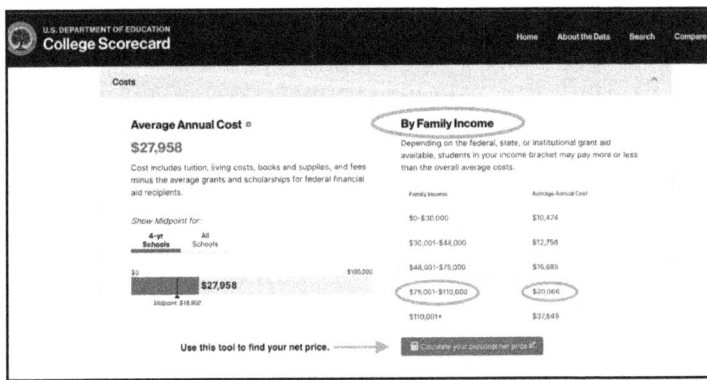

Source: collegescorecard.ed.gov

CHAPTER 5: Strategy #3: Chase the Money—Generous Colleges

However, one of the best ways to find colleges that offer generous financial aid is collegedata.com. You can search colleges based on the amount of financial need they meet and even learn the percentage of students receiving merit aid.

As a reminder, your demonstrated financial need is the estimated minimum amount a college determines you can pay based on the information you provided in the FAFSA (or the CSS Profile for some private colleges). Upon completing the FAFSA, you will receive a FSS with your SAI—a number that could start at -$1,500 and go as high as the full cost of attending the college. (Remember, the SAI was formerly called the EFC.)

So, if your SAI/EFC is the estimated minimum amount your family must come up with, what about the rest? Well, if a college has generous financial aid, it will provide you with a package that covers the rest or the balance of the COA, ideally without too many loans. A small number of colleges claim to meet 100 percent of a family's demonstrated financial need; an even smaller number meet 100 percent of a family's demonstrated financial need without loans. Most colleges will not meet 100 percent of your family's financial need.

To find colleges that meet close to 100 percent (maybe 90 to 100 percent) of demonstrated financial need, visit collegedata.com.

Here is how to use the tool to find colleges that meet close to 100 percent of financial need:

1. Go to www.collegedata.com.
2. On the homepage, click the "College Search" tab.
3. On the search page, find a section called "Financials, Debt & Aid."
4. Under "Financials, Debt & Aid," go to "Financial Needs Met."
5. Move the dial from zero to one hundred and review the list of colleges. You can move the dial away from 100 percent to find more colleges. (Remember the closer to 100 percent of financial need a college meets, the more generous they are. This usually means fewer out-of-pocket costs for you.)
6. Click on any of the colleges ("save school") to view a description that will tell you more about that college. To get more information, you'll have to create an account.

Here are a few things to keep in mind:
- To find colleges that award large merit aid packages, uncheck the box "Only include students without financial need" if you are searching for need-based aid.
- Collegedata.com allows you to find colleges based on many criteria, including financial need met, merit aid, entrance difficulty, graduation rate, COA, and majors, to name a few.
- On the website, take some time to play around with

the different features and you will be able to build a list of colleges that offer the most generous aid.

BUILDING YOUR COLLEGE LIST

When creating a college list, students should consider their likelihood of acceptance as well as the affordability of each option. As the results of applications can be unpredictable, it is important to apply to a range of colleges—some that are a bit of a challenge, some that are an ideal fit, and some that are considered a "safety" and almost guarantee admission.

Building a college list means considering several different factors, including your student's interests, academic profile, and preferences in location, college size, and of course, affordability. Ideally, students should build a list of no more than ten to twelve colleges including ones that could be considered safety colleges, match colleges, and reach (less likely) colleges.

Cost should be a significant factor when deciding on a college. In the end, you not only want your student to land where they'll thrive but where you can afford the education. Financing a college education shouldn't become another stressor. Think back to when you settled in a neighborhood with your young family and remember that the same principles used to select your home will apply to college choice. Like that move, a college search should list preferences. For example, during your home search, you likely researched school districts, low crime rates, amenities, parks, and costs. However, as much as you fell in love with the charm of a neighborhood, if the home price was higher than you could afford, you had to move on and find another place.

KEY TAKEAWAYS

To keep your college costs down, find colleges that are affordable. Affordability, however, doesn't always start with the sticker price. A college that lists a high cost of attendance (COA) on its website could end up being the most affordable for your family if they offer generous financial aid.

Learn how to find generous colleges and then build a college list that includes a few of them. There is no guarantee that your student will get in, but that is the reality of college admissions. However, you must be in it to win it, so if they don't apply, they will not have a chance.

Use collegedata.com to find and compare colleges with generous financial aid, keeping in mind that most colleges do not meet 100 percent of need (learn more about financial need in Chapter 3).

CHAPTER 6:
Strategy #4: Apply for Access

A college access program is like the key that unlocks your dreams.

College access programs can help to reduce your college costs. They provide free services and resources to students from low-income families or first-generation college-goers. The services and resources include tutoring, college counseling, test prep, career guidance, and, in some cases, scholarships. A few programs like Posse and Questbridge offer full-tuition and full-ride scholarships through their college partners. As a result, it is very competitive to get in. Both programs seek highly motivated, academically strong students, preparing them for top-tier colleges and universities.

College access programs serve to close the education gap between these students and other students.

While I can't speak for all college access programs, those like Posse and QuestBridge have partnered with some of the most selective colleges in the country, such as Brown, Princeton, and Vanderbilt. Students who go through these programs are often matched with a college and almost guaranteed a spot.

HOW TO FIND A COLLEGE ACCESS PROGRAM

Keep in mind, not all college access programs offer scholarships. Therefore, you'll need to do some research to find the ones that do, including both the large, well-known ones and the small, local programs. However, don't overlook those programs that don't offer scholarships. For example, while Matriculate, College Point, and College Advising Corps may not provide scholarships, they do offer personalized college guidance, college application assistance, and mentoring services. These resources could potentially enhance your child's competitiveness for scholarships from colleges or private organizations.

To find other college access programs in your area, visit the Coalition for College database of college access and success programs around the United States at https://www.coalitionforcollegeaccess.org/cbo-id. You can search by name, city, and state. There is also an advanced search feature.

Another place to look is in your child's school counselor's office. They will be very familiar with students who might have gone through these programs.

TWO TOP COLLEGE ACCESS PROGRAMS IN THE UNITED STATES

1. POSSE

Posse is a college access program that focuses on providing mentoring and educational support to select groups of underrepresented students. The program identifies high-achieving students from public high schools with limited resources and provides them with a full-tuition scholarship to one of the Posse partner colleges or universities. Posse students are actively involved in the college application process and receive ongoing mentoring, workshops, and college counseling to ensure their success. The program aims to increase the number of minority students attending top-tier universities and graduating with a college degree.

―――――――― *Partner Colleges* ――――――――

The Posse Foundation is a scholarship program that was created in 1989 by Deborah Bial. It was established to identify and support highly motivated students from different backgrounds. The students, who attend college in small groups known as "Posses," are provided with tuition assistance and mentoring to help them succeed in college and beyond.

The Posse Foundation partners with more than sixty colleges, including Brown, Cornell, Texas A&M, and Vanderbilt. Students who are selected (Posse Scholars) receive a full four-year tuition scholarship. They also receive mentoring throughout the program. While in college, students in the "Posse" provide each other with peer support.

The Posse Foundation works with partner universities to recruit students from around the country who demonstrate strong leadership potential and academic success.

To apply for a Posse Foundation scholarship, students must first submit an online application. Once the application is submitted, the Posse Foundation reviews the applications and selects the finalists. The finalists are then invited to participate in interviews, group activities, and other assessments.

If your student is selected as a scholar, they will receive a comprehensive college prep program that includes workshops in team-building, leadership, cross-cultural communication, and academics.

When students arrive on campus, they continue to receive support through mentors and retreats to ensure they persist and graduate.

Posse is currently recruiting students who attend public high schools and community-based organizations in the following ten cities (Posse Foundation, n.d.). They

also offer a virtual program for students outside of these metropolitan areas.
1. Posse New York
2. Posse Atlanta
3. Posse Bay Area
4. Posse Boston
5. Posse Chicago
6. Posse DC
7. Posse Houston
8. Posse Los Angeles
9. Posse Miami
10. Posse New Orleans

--- *How to Apply* ---

To apply, your student must be a high school junior or senior and be nominated by their counselor or other community organization leader. They must demonstrate leadership in their high school, community, or family and have good academic potential.

For more information, please visit the Posse Foundation's website: posseefoundation.org.

2. QUESTBRIDGE

QuestBridge is another well-known college access program. It provides full scholarships for bright students from low-income backgrounds. Through partnerships, this program helps to match high achieving high school students to top colleges and universities.

QuestBridge also provides financial aid packages, mentoring, and support services to ensure that students can successfully transition to college. The program also offers virtual mentoring and college counseling as well as college tours and fairs to help students make informed decisions about their college choice. QuestBridge provides an invaluable opportunity to students who may not have otherwise considered attending a top-tier college or university.

QuestBridge partners with some of the best colleges in the country. Students who are part of this program go on to colleges like Brown, Dartmouth, Tufts, Wellesley, Penn, Notre Dame, Columbia, Bowdoin, Chicago, Yale, Washington (St. Louis), and Southern California, among others.

They have two programs: National College Match and College Prep Scholars Program.

Students joining the program as high school juniors could be awarded a full scholarship to a college summer program at Yale, Emory, University of Chicago, or another partner school.

Selected students may also have opportunities to visit college partner campuses, get college essay feedback, receive an award for a new laptop, and access resources to strengthen their college application.

Partner Colleges

QuestBridge partners with slightly under fifty colleges, including most of the Ivy League schools. Participating colleges include Amherst, Brown, Claremont McKenna, Colorado College, Dartmouth, Duke, Emory, and the Massachusetts Institute of Technology.

If your student is a high school junior in the top 5 to 10 percent of their class and from a family earning no more than $65,000 per year (as of August 2023), they should apply. Their family's assets and other household circumstances are also considered. QuestBridge recruits mostly straight-A students with "evidence of strong writing ability, intellectual spark, and determination" (Questbridge, n.d.).

The program takes a very holistic approach when reviewing applicants. In addition to grades, curriculum, accomplishments, and financial need, it also looks at other factors, such as a student's personal circumstances, the parents' level of education, and the student's family responsibilities.

How to Apply

To apply for a fully funded four-year scholarship, your student must submit an online application. Please visit QuestBridge for more information on how to apply at questbridge.org.

KEY TAKEAWAYS

A college access program can help reduce college costs by providing resources to make the process of applying to college more successful. College access programs can offer services like mentors and college preparation classes.

Here are some things you can do:
1. Learn more about Posse and QuestBridge to see if your student meets the criteria.
2. Find other college access programs in your area by visiting https://www.coalitionforcollegeaccess.org/cbo-id. You can search by name, city, and state.

CHAPTER 7:
Strategy #5: A Degree at Half Price—Collegiate High School

Getting an associate degree while completing high school may seem like a lot of work, but it's worth the effort; you get two diplomas for the price of one!

Did you know you could begin saving for college even before your student gets to college—and is still in high school?

Early collegiate high schools are an increasingly popular option for students looking to reduce the cost of college. These schools provide the same rigorous academic curriculum as traditional high schools but with the added benefit of allowing students to complete college-level courses and earn an associate degree upon graduation. Students earn college credits and get a head start on their college education, saving money in the long run.

By taking college-level courses in high school, students can save thousands of dollars on tuition and fees and save time by taking fewer classes in college.

COLLEGIATE HIGH SCHOOL

In the spring of 2008, my spouse at the time received a transfer to Dallas, Texas. I can't say I was thrilled about it, although I had great memories of an earlier visit to Dallas. You see, I'm an "over-researcher" by nature, so once I started googling Dallas and learning more about the area, I started getting heart palpitations about the fact that it is right smack in the middle of tornado alley. "I can't go there," I thought. I had seen too much devastation from tornadoes on the news.

After a few days of trying to convince my husband to not take the assignment (to no avail), I settled in for the adventure. I was going to get ready to make the most of this assignment like I had when we were assigned to Papua New Guinea or Congo. Prepare! Prepare! Prepare! And it wasn't like we were going to a whole different country.

Part of the preparation included looking for good schools for my two daughters to attend. They had more than their fair share of moves under their young belts, and I had to ensure they were placed in an environment where

CHAPTER 7: Strategy #5: A Degree at Half Price—Collegiate High School

they would strive—one that provided the same level of support and academic challenge they were used to. We wrote a short list of a few well-known private schools in the Dallas-Fort Worth area.

My daughters applied and were accepted to two of the finest private schools in Dallas: The Hockaday School and Greenhill School. We were elated when they were accepted since the competition to get in was similar to applying to college. I mean, my daughters had to do a standardized test, write essays, and be interviewed. We decided to visit the schools in Dallas over my daughters' spring break before committing to any one school. During one half-day visit to The Hockaday School, I went to check out the local public school—just in case. I visited Highland Park High School, one of the best public schools in Dallas (due in part to the wealthy area).

While I was touring the beautiful campus, I picked up a brochure that provided information on where students could take college credits at Dallas College. I then went to my phone and began looking up Dallas College. I searched and found the college online and stumbled upon a website that advertised a collegiate high school. At that time, I had little or no knowledge of what a collegiate high school was. This piqued my interest.

Once I shared the program with my daughters, they were immediately interested in applying. They loved both Hockaday and Greenhill, but they were painfully familiar with some of the challenges with trying to break into friend groups and cliques, especially if students had known each other for years. Richland Collegiate High School, they thought, would help them bypass any of the challenges or trauma of trying to fit in. Again. The program was for students entering eleventh grade, and students could come from any school district. Everyone in the collegiate high school would be new to the school. They applied to Richland Collegiate High School, and got in.

As a result of my daughters attending a collegiate high school, we saved more than $100,000. My daughters graduated from high school two years later with an associate degree and a high school diploma. When they applied to colleges as seniors, they won admission into colleges that spanned the range of selectivity, including Vanderbilt, Texas A&M, and Southern Methodist University. They were able to complete their bachelor's degrees in two years and two-and-a-half years (due to studying abroad). They went on to earn master's degrees at the same time many of their friends were just earning their bachelor's degrees.

This is one of many success stories of attending a two-year early college program and successfully completing college. Of course, you must understand your values to commit to one of these nontraditional programs. Some feel going to an elite or brand-name program is the only way to go or success is not possible. I am here to tell you otherwise. As you consider financing college, your values will come into play—how you feel about what others think of you, whether you need to keep up with the Joneses, or whether you are OK with going against the grain to achieve what's right for you and your family. The media and some of your peers might consider anything but elite schools a failure. You have to know your values and stick to them.

WHAT IS AN EARLY COLLEGE HIGH SCHOOL? (THE HISTORY)

Early college high schools, a bit of a new phenomenon, can save families tens of thousands of dollars. The appearance of most of these programs go back to 2002, when the Gates Foundation donated $40 million as part of a Gates Foundation Early College initiative. Some similar programs have been around since the 1990s.

The program is different from dual credits, which allows students to earn high school credits and college credits in some subjects. Early college high schools allow students to earn their high school diploma at the same time they are earning an associate degree. The program is usually sponsored by a two-year or four-year college, and the programs take place on the college's campus. The programs can run from eleventh to twelfth grade, or from ninth through twelfth grades.

The idea behind these schools was to create smaller high school programs to give students from disadvantaged backgrounds a chance to succeed and go on to college. The maximum number of students in each program would be four hundred; however, many are smaller. My daughters' high school class was under two hundred students.

While some of these programs target students from disadvantaged backgrounds who are not as likely to attend college, the student body often includes students from all backgrounds. It's not uncommon to find students from upper-middle-class backgrounds in these programs. In fact, I would proffer that most parents are not aware that these programs were set up to target a specific demographic, and it is often not widely advertised. Most people just hear about them from a friend or the local news and become interested in learning more.

Early college high schools or collegiate high schools typically start in eleventh grade but can start sooner. In Texas, you will find both residential and nonresidential programs. My daughters attended a nonresidential program.

One well-known residential early college high school is the University of North Texas's Texas Academy of Mathematics and Science. It is the first program of its kind in the United States and is geared toward high-achieving students. Students must be a Texas resident to apply and come from one of the area's high schools. SAT or ACT scores must accompany the applications. While

CHAPTER 7: Strategy #5: A Degree at Half Price—Collegiate High School

most of the early college programs are free, the fee to attend this residential program can reach over $27,000. However, each student must fill out and submit the FAFSA to become eligible for one of the scholarships based on financial need. In programs like these, students are exposed to research alongside the university's professors and undergraduate and graduate students.

Some programs can be quite competitive. In many programs, there are more applicants than there are spots available in the program. In those cases, students are often selected based on a lottery.

Since the early 2000s, many states have followed this model. Texas is one of the states that is leading this trend. By giving high school students the opportunity to earn an associate degree (two years' worth of college) at no cost to families, it can significantly reduce the overall cost of college.

Not every student is ideal for this program. It is extremely rigorous. In addition, most programs may not offer organized after-school clubs and activities. Students must take the initiative to join clubs either on the college campus (if opened to them) or independent clubs or start their own projects.

Most of these programs take place on a college campus, and students attend classes with other traditional college students who graduated high school the traditional way over four years. They have the same amount of freedom as college students. In addition, they are taught by professors who might not keep up with their attendance. The level of independence might work for some students who are responsible. However, some may flounder and fail.

My daughters were in, I believe, the second cohort for the school, which means only one class beofre theirs had completed the program and simultaneously earned their high school and college degrees. As a result, there were still some unknowns. I remember sitting through an information session and still couldn't understand how they were going to complete high school and college at the same time. The administrators did not do the best job of presenting the information. Due to some of those early coordination challenges, my daughters ended up with more than twenty credits above what was required for an associate degree. The program was new, and there were a lot of kinks that needed to be worked out. Since then, however, students no longer take as many credits.

IS AN EARLY COLLEGE HIGH SCHOOL RIGHT FOR YOUR STUDENT?

If your child is a highly motivated and independent student, they will do well in these programs. Students in these programs generally have a heavy academic workload; they might be doing upward of fifteen credits per semester. Since they are technically college students, they might not receive the same amount of hand-holding as in high schools. Yes, advisors are available, and some programs have parent-teacher groups. I actually served as vice president and president of the PTA during my daughters' time at the school.

If your child wants to play sports at the collegiate level, a collegiate high school might not be the best fit. They may not get the same opportunities to join sports teams as they would in a traditional high school. Also, it's worth noting that not every community college fields a football team. Of course, athletics vary from school to school and things change over time.

Here are some qualities that are essential for a student to succeed at one of these schools:
- Strong academics
- Highly organized
- Great time-management skills
- Highly motivated
- OK with not playing varsity sports (differs from program to program)
- Open to making new friends
- Comfortable with change
- Ability to advocate for themselves

WHAT ARE ADVANTAGES OF THIS PROGRAM?

If your child graduates from an early college high school, you can save tens of thousands of dollars. However, it also provides added benefits. It helps students with the transition to college, increasing the likelihood that they will graduate from college.

Many of the early college high schools have special partnerships with four-year colleges and will often provide full or partial scholarships for students who transfer into their program.

Students graduating from early college high schools are more likely to go to a four-year college and graduate. Studies conducted by the Community College Research Center indicate that students entering a four-year college with a significant number of credits have a higher likelihood of completing their college education.[16]

Early college high school graduates are also much more prepared to advocate for themselves. They have already gained experience in navigating a college setting. These programs do offer some support, but the level of support is often less than you might find in a typical high school.

These programs can also provide a boost to a student's confidence. A student who has already been exposed to two years of college work will feel ready to tackle two additional years in college.

Most early college high school programs are affiliated with a particular two- or four-year college, which makes transferring credits to a bachelor's degree an easy process in most cases. The early college high school program in your state will more than likely be familiar to the universities in your state and even some out of state. It's

CHAPTER 7: Strategy #5: A Degree at Half Price—Collegiate High School

not a bad idea to check with the colleges your student might be interested in attending to find out if they will accept all their credits.

Going the early college high school route could save you up to two years' worth of college costs.

HOW DO I FIND AN EARLY COLLEGE PROGRAM?

The best way to find an early college high school in your state is to check your state's department of education website for a list of early college high schools in your area. You can also search for "early college high schools [your state]" to find more detailed information.

Additionally, you can talk to your student's school counselor or contact your local school district and ask about early college high school programs in your area.

States such as Texas, Tennessee, and New York are leading the way in early college high schools. According to *U.S. News & World Report*, as of 2022, there were four hundred of these programs throughout the United States.[17]

HOW TO APPLY FOR ADMISSION

The admissions requirement of each school will be different. Check with the specific program your student is interested in attending.

As a rule, collegiate high schools or early college high schools tend to attract students with a broader range of academic abilities. However, don't let this fool you into thinking it's an easy path to getting two years knocked off your student's college years.

On the contrary, it's quite rigorous and demands a great deal of organizational and time-management skills to stay on top of all the courses your student will be taking. While these programs offer more support than they might get if they were already in college, have no doubt about it, your student must become familiar with navigating the available resources and advocate for themselves.

Some programs like Richland Collegiate High School in Dallas admit students entering eleventh grade. So, the ideal time to begin looking into these programs is when your student is in ninth grade, or at the latest, in tenth grade since the applications have to be submitted while your student is still a sophomore.

Begin having the conversation with your student in ninth grade. If they respond favorably to the idea, arrange a visit early to get a feel for the school and see if it is a good fit. Some students are eager to finish high school with a college degree. Others just want to get away from the social scene at their current high school, so they see early college high school as a great opportunity to do so.

If you decide that a collegiate high school is right for your student, keep in mind they may have to seek out extracurricular activities and sporting activities elsewhere. Many of these schools might not offer the same volume of after-school programs as a typical high school. However, this shouldn't be a deal-breaker because you could work with your child to develop ideas for an after-school activity, whether it's starting a business or a nonprofit or joining some type of sport league that is open to all kids their age. There are also many opportunities to volunteer in your community no matter which school your student attends, traditional or nontraditional.

KEY TAKEAWAYS

Early college high school can play a significant role in reducing your overall college costs. It allows your student to get two years of college out of the way, and then you'll only have to pay for the final two toward an undergraduate degree.

To find early college high schools in your area:
1. Use Google or check with the department of education in your state to find early college high schools.
2. Once you find them, visit a couple of schools to see if the programs are a good fit for your student. Initially, it might feel like your student has to give up a lot in terms of extracurricular activities (many have limited extracurricular activities); only you and your child can decide whether that loss is worth the trade-off.

While these programs are not for everyone, there is often more to gain than to lose if you believe your child can thrive in this academic setting.

CHAPTER 8:
Strategy #6: Start Out at a Two-Year College

Starting college at a community college is a great way to get a good education at a more affordable price and still have money for pizza and fun.

Are you looking for a way to avoid amassing student debt? Consider having your child start their college career at a community college. There are some clear benefits of attending a community college and then transferring to a four-year college. Some of these benefits include lower costs and the ability to strengthen their academic record.

Starting at a two-year college could cut your college costs in half. Your student could knock out their first two years of college and then transfer to a four-year university to complete their bachelor's degree. If you feel you want to save money or maybe you're not sure they're ready for a four-year college, look at the junior college in your town.

However, don't rule out a four-year college until you have done your research. Some four-year colleges charge zero tuition if your family income is under a certain amount.

If your student plans to pursue a career that requires only an associate degree, a two-year college is a *no-brainer*.

Unfortunately, community colleges can sometimes get a bad rap as slightly inferior versions of four-year-colleges. However, that is not true. Some graduates of two-year colleges even get into Ivy League schools. "Among all students who completed a degree at a four-year college in 2015–16, 49 percent had enrolled at a two-year college in the previous ten years," says the Community College Research Center at Columbia University.[18]

Following are some benefits of attending a two-year college.

1. LOWER TUITION

You will pay significantly less money for your child to attend a two-year college than you would for them to be freshman and sophomores at a four-year college. You could easily save one-third of overall college costs.

According to EducationData.org, the average annual tuition for the 2022–23 school year was $3,501 for a two-year college, while a four-year college charged $9,377 (tuition and fees only). If we consider the additional cost of room and board at a four-year public institution, averaging $16,650 per year, it becomes evident that opting for a two plus two path is a winner. By attending a two-year college, more students can reside at home, resulting in significantly lower expenses for food and housing.

Some community colleges are upping their game by offering a limited number of bachelor's degrees. This makes it possible for some students to graduate without having to transfer. For example, Collin County Community College in Texas offers two bachelor's degrees at the same per-credit cost as an associate degree. Students are now able complete bachelor's degrees in nursing and technology for under $10,000.

2. FREE COLLEGE

Another benefit of going to a community college is the fact that it might actually be free. Two-year colleges in sixteen states, including Texas, offer last-dollar promise programs. These last-dollar programs cover the tuition not covered by other grants and scholarships.

Dallas County Promise, for example, is available for seniors graduating from participating high schools in Dallas County. Students from over eighty participating high schools (as of December 2023) can benefit from the The Dallas County Promise (https://dallascountypromise.org/) program.

Students in the program can transfer into a participating four-year college and receive the same scholarship. There is even an option to start out at some of the partner four-year universities.

3. ASSOCIATE DEGREE CAREERS

If your student is interested in a career that only requires an associate degree, this is a perfect option for you. Your student will be able to earn credentials without amassing too much student debt.

Here is a sampling of high-paying jobs in the science, technology, engineering, and math (STEM) field, as well as the health field, that can be pursued with an associate degree and their corresponding average annual earnings:

- Radiation therapist: $82,790
- Occupational therapy assistant: $61,520
- Respiratory therapist: $61,830
- Web developer: $79,890
- Computer network support specialist $76,060
- Dental hygienist: $77,810
- Registered nurse: $77,600[19]

4. TIME TO ADJUST

Community college also offers time to adjust to college life.

Sadly, many students leave home for a four-year college ill-prepared for the challenges of an independent life. However, beginning with a two-year college will help make it an easier transition.

To succeed in college, your student must commit to building good time-management and study skills and advocating for themselves. Starting out at a two-year school could help your child strengthen the skills needed to attend and graduate from college.

5. ACADEMIC RECORD IMPROVEMENT

A study cited in a *Harvard Graduate School of Education* article found that "only 32 percent of students leave high school academically prepared for college. This percentage is even lower among Black and Hispanic students."[20] Given these statistics, it is not surprising that many students who start college will drop out. The students who face the greatest burden are those who drop out without a degree and with tens of thousands of dollars in student debt.

If your child's high school academic record is less than stellar, starting at a community college might be right for them. They could strengthen their academic record before transferring.

Additionally, they can take remedial courses without incurring the high costs of a four-year college. If they are on the academic cusp, starting at a community college will teach them how to manage a full workload before moving to a four-year college.

AVOIDING PITFALLS

Although one of the benefits of attending a community college is lower student debt, there are some potential pitfalls. If your student is not vigilant, they could end up taking more credits than they need. Or they could miss taking the required credits for transfer to a specific bachelor's degree program.

To avoid these pitfalls, they should meet with their advisor on a regular basis. Scheduling a meeting before they register for courses each semester will ensure they are on track for graduation. If they plan to transfer to a four-year college, they should talk to advisors both at their current and prospective colleges.

Here are a few questions to ask both advisors:
- How many credits can I transfer?
- What is the minimum GPA required for credits to transfer?
- Does the college have an articulation (transfer) agreement with any four-year colleges?
- Is there a residency requirement (required number of credits taken at the four-year college) for graduation?

A successful transfer to a four-year college will require significant vigilance on your student's part.

One note of caution. Before your student decides to pursue an education at a two-year college, do some homework. Compare different college options to ensure it is indeed the best value and the best option for your child.

If your student is considering a two plus two track (community college then four-year college), ask yourself "Where can my student get the best education for the least amount of money?" A two-year college is a good option, but it is not for everyone. However, if your student is driven to succeed and remains focused on their goals, they will become one of the many success stories of this option.

KEY TAKEAWAYS

The biggest benefit of having your child start their college career at a two-year college is the amount of money you will save. And in many states, students can attend community college for free.

Besides cost, two-year colleges are the perfect place for your student to boost their academic record and adjust to the rigors of college before transferring to a four-year university.

Of course, the choice to attend a two-year college is a no-brainer if your child is interested in a career that only requires two years or less of college. For example, some high-paying STEM and healthcare careers like registered nurse, web developer, or radiation therapist might only require an associate degree.

Despite the many benefits of a two-year college, one of the biggest pitfalls students may face is losing credits when transferring from a two- to a four-year college.

And what, you may ask, is the solution to this? Well, one of the best solutions is to have your student meet regularly with their advisor and review the policy of the four-year college they plan to transfer to before registering for classes.

CHAPTER 9:
Strategy #7: Tuition-Free Programs and Colleges

―――――――――

Education should never be a privilege exclusive to a few, for it holds the power to transform lives and build a better world for everyone.

To help more students go to college, a number of states and institutions provide tuition-free education. Some programs allow students to attend two-year colleges tuition-free, while many more programs are available to students attending a four-year college. These programs are usually considered a last-dollar scholarship, meaning they are meant to cover the tuition (or other) costs not covered by any federal or state financial aid you are eligible to receive.

These programs are usually advertised on colleges' websites and might be listed as a grant or a scholarship and may or may not contain the words "tuition-free" in them. However, you will usually find eligibility requirements to help you figure out if you qualify and determine if it is, indeed, a "tuition-free" program.

The first true tuition-free program in the United States was in the state of California. In 1975, California's Board of Regents introduced the Cal Grant program, which allows low-income high school students to attend any college or university in the state without having to pay tuition.

The second of the 1970s free-tuition programs was the New York State Tuition Assistance Program (TAP), which went into effect in 1978. This program provides financial support to New York state residents pursuing a degree at a college or university. The 1980s and 1990s saw more programs develop, such as the Maryland Free Tuition Program of 1988, which was one of the first to include a tuition waiver for higher education students.

In recent years, the tuition-free trend has been growing in the United States. Such programs allow students from any background or financial situation to get the education they need from colleges and universities tuition-free. These programs may or may not cover books and fees, and very few cover the cost of accommodations. Most of the tuition-free programs have an income eligibility criterion, while a few are open to any student from that state or county. Some private

CHAPTER 9: Strategy #7: Tuition-Free Programs and Colleges

colleges also have tuition-free programs. Those are more likely to be open to out-of-state students.

According to a study from the Center for American Progress, nearly "two-thirds of high school graduates who attended a tuition-free college program said they would not have been able to attend college without the opportunity."[21] Programs like the New York Excelsior Scholarship and Washington's College Bound program have helped countless students attend college without having to take on significant debt.

This trend is growing in popularity, and more states are now offering tuition-free college programs to their residents every year. For many students, the idea of tuition-free college is a life-changing opportunity. Not only does it give them the chance to attend college without the stress of paying for it, but it also helps open up their career paths and job opportunities. This is particularly important for students from low-income families who might otherwise have to forgo college.

Programs like New York's Excelsior Scholarship and California's Cal Grant are providing opportunities for tuition-free college. The Excelsior Scholarship, for example, covers tuition costs for students whose family income is less than $125,000. It also awards funds for books and supplies. On the other hand, the Cal Grant program provides funds for tuition as well as living expenses, such as housing and food. Another trend related to tuition-free college programs is the growing number of community colleges that are offering free tuition.

There are approximately eighty community colleges across the United States that offer free tuition programs. And currently, thirty-two states in the US offer free college programs according to the Campaign for Free College Tuition.[22] Tennessee was the first to implement this in 2014, followed by Oregon in 2015.

Texas has also been leading the way in free-tuition programs at the county level and at individual universities. Here are three such colleges in Texas.

1. UNIVERSITY OF TEXAS AT AUSTIN | AUSTIN

Texas Advance Commitment (https://texasadvance.utexas.edu/): In 2020, the university began offering free tuition to students with household income of $65,000 or less. The university also provides partial tuition support for families earning up to $125,000.

2. DALLAS COLLEGE DISTRICT | DALLAS

Dallas County Promise (https://dallascountypromise.org/): This free-tuition program is available to high school graduates from sixty-five-plus participating Promise High Schools in Dallas County. It covers the cost of tuition not paid by federal and state financial aid.

3. RICE UNIVERSITY | HOUSTON

The Rice Investment https://financialaid.rice.edu/rice-investment: Rice University, a highly selective private university, offers some of the most generous financial aid to low- and middle-income families. Rice expanded this program in 2021, and students with a family income below $75,000 will now receive funds to cover full tuition, fees, room, and board. Students from families with incomes between $75,000 and $140,000 get their full tuition covered.

In addition, Rice University is also one of only a few colleges that is considered a no-loan university. This means if your student is fortunate enough to be accepted and is eligible for financial aid, they will receive a financial aid package without any loans.

In March 2023, Georgia's lawmakers agreed to expand the HOPE scholarship to cover 100 percent of students' tuition at a public university. This is good news for students in that state. Students must maintain a 3.0 GPA and apply using the FAFSA.

HOW TO FIND TUITION-FREE COLLEGES AND PROGRAMS

To learn more about your state's financial aid program, visit the National Association of Student Financial Aid Administrator (NASFAA) website (https://www.nasfaa.org/State_Financial_Aid_Programs).

Click on your state on the map to learn about the programs that you might be able to take advantage of.

Most of these programs have a residency requirement. If your student is interested in attending a university in a neighboring state, check the State and Regional College Tuition Exchanges (https://www.nasfaa.org/State_Regional_Tuition_Exchanges) for any regional discount program that allows students to attend college in another state and still pay in-state tuition.

Another good way to way to find tuition-free colleges and programs is by checking out the financial aid section of a college's website. Your student's high school counselor is another great resource, as they might have a list of colleges with these programs in place. The financial aid advisor at the college your student plans to attend would also have this information. If your student is nervous about calling before applying, they could just call and ask a general question without even providing their name.

10 SMALL, TUITION-FREE COLLEGES

Before I end this chapter, let me share the names of ten small, not-so-well-known colleges that allow students to attend for free. While these colleges may not have the same name recognition as those often mentioned in the news, they might be an excellent financial, educational, and social fit for your child. Some are work colleges, meaning students participate in on-campus work to help pay for their education.

CHAPTER 9: Strategy #7: Tuition-Free Programs and Colleges

It is important to note attending a tuition-free college does not mean it is entirely free. You may still have to pay for food and housing (room and board). Each college has its own eligibility criteria.

1. Berea College (Kentucky)
2. Barclay College (Kansas)
3. Cooper Union (New York—returning to tuition-free education in 2029)
4. Alice Lloyd College (Kentucky)
5. University of the Ozarks (Arkansas)
6. College of the Ozarks (Missouri)
7. Curtis Institute of Music (Pennsylvania)
8. Sterling College (Vermont)
9. Warren Wilson College (North Carolina)
10. Webb Institute (New York)

KEY TAKEAWAYS

Tuition-free colleges and programs abound. And while many are geared toward families from low-income backgrounds, some are available to middle-income families too.

These programs are a great way to reduce your costs, although they might not cover fees and accommodations. However, if you are eligible for the program, you could end up saving a lot, especially if your student is living at home while going to school.

To find out if you qualify, have your student:
- Visit NASFAA to find financial aid programs in your state.
- Talk to their high school counselor.
- Talk to the financial aid officer at the college(s) they plan to attend.

CHAPTER 10:
Strategy #8: Consider the Military

To serve in the military is to embody selflessness, embracing the essence of duty and sacrifice.

Eliminating college costs could boil down to your student serving the country. If they are interested in military service, attending a military academy or joining the Corps of Cadets or Reserved Officers Training Corps (ROTC) offered at hundreds of colleges could significantly reduce your costs or erase them altogether. Be aware that this arrangement will require a set number of years of service from your student.

Some students pursue the ROTC out of a deep sense of calling or a desire to uphold a long-standing family tradition. These individuals see it as an opportunity to honor a sense of duty and contribute to a legacy that is important to them.

One young student I worked with was intent on joining ROTC. For him, it was a matter of tradition. I met Peter when he was preparing to take the SAT or ACT but wasn't sure which one to take, so I set up a time to meet Peter at my office for an assessment. When he arrived, we sat down for a chat while the instructors prepared the test. I asked him about his dream college, and without hesitation he blurted out: "I want to attend Texas A&M" and "I want to join the corps."

"OK, this is good," I thought, "a student who knows what they want is always a plus."

I said, "Peter, that's great. Texas A&M is a great college, and based on what you want to study, you will have many opportunities for research there."

"Yes, m'am," he responded. "I've always wanted to join the military." He went on to tell me about a proud and long line of service in his family that wove back generations.

For Peter, the ROTC option was the best fit.

The US service academies or ROTC programs are great options for students who want to serve their country. However, your student should weigh all the pros and cons of joining before deciding this is the best path to reduce college costs. If they attend one of the academies, they commit to serve in the military upon graduation. It is a bit different with ROTC programs, as it depends on the path your student chooses or the scholarships they accept.

CHAPTER 10: Strategy #8: Consider the Military

THE FEDERAL SERVICE ACADEMIES: MILITARY ACADEMIES

Did you know that the military academies pay students to attend? Well, more like pay students while they attend. One of the biggest benefits of attending is that your student will receive a full-ride scholarship. Additionally, cadets receive a stipend, free accommodations, and three or four square meals daily.

However, before your student runs off to begin applying, they should be aware that the programs are quite rigorous, both academically and physically. And upon graduation, your student must commit to serve in the military for eight years.

There are five federal service academies:
1. US Military Academy, West Point, New York
2. US Naval Academy, Annapolis, Maryland
3. US Air Force Academy, Colorado Springs, Colorado
4. US Coast Guard Academy, New London, Connecticut
5. US Merchant Marine Academy, Kings Point, New York

The academies are highly regarded institutions of higher learning, and as such, they are very competitive to get into. The White House website describes ideal candidates for the US military academies in the following words: "It takes a well-rounded program of leadership, academic, and athletic preparation to be one of the few who can meet the Service Academies' high admission standards and the fierce competition for appointment."[23]

If your student plans to attend, they should take a college prep curriculum in high school and practice for the ACT and SAT exams. Most of the cadets at the academies are in the top 25 percent of their high school class. According to the Air Force website, its students are in the top 3 percent of their class.

Your student will not only be expected to have the academic chops to get in, but they'll also have to show a record of leadership and prove that they are physically fit. Candidates must take a series of physical fitness assessments, including sit-ups, push-ups and a one-mile run.

Again, the academies are quite rigorous. If your student is accepted, they can expect a very challenging academic and physical program. Cadets undergo intensive leadership training, preparing them for leadership roles in the military.

HOW TO GET IN

Preparation to join the academies should begin as early as the fall of your student's junior year in high school. All of the academies have academic, physical, and medical requirements.

Getting into a U.S. service academy is a two-step process. First, the student applies directly to the academy of their choice, which involves a comprehensive evaluation of their character, leadership, physical aptitude, medical fitness, and motivation. Second, the student seeks a nomination from a U.S. Senator, Representative, or the Vice President, which requires submitting documents like SAT or ACT scores, teacher recommendation letters, transcripts, resumes, etc. Some offices also conduct interviews for applicants. It's worth noting that students can apply to more than one service academy to increase their chances of receiving a nomination.

Applicants must be between seventeen and twenty-three and unmarried without any dependents.

To learn more about each academy's admission requirements, please visit their website:

1. US Military Academy (https://www.westpoint.edu/)
2. US Naval Academy (https://www.usna.edu/homepage.php)
3. US Coast Guard Academy (https://uscga.edu/)
4. US Merchant Marine Academy (https://www.usmma.edu/)
5. US Air Force Academy (https://www.usafa.af.mil/)

COMMITMENT TO MILITARY UPON GRADUATION

As the saying goes, "No one gets a free ride." Well, it's the same for the military. Upon graduation, your student must serve a total of eight years in the military—five years of active duty and three years in the reserves. This is one of the main reasons your student should consider their motives when applying to an academy. Getting a free college education should not be their only motivation.

In addition to time commitment, your student will have to commit to the military lifestyle. This means they must follow strict rules and regulations and participate in military drills and activities. If they are not good with structure, this might not be the best option for them.

THE CORPS OF CADETS AND ROTC OPTION

An additional route to getting full or partial scholarships is through other military options, either through the Corps of Cadets or ROTC. Both programs offer your student a path to the military and financial help to pay for college. Depending on the scholarships your student accepts and the path they choose, they may have to commit to serve in the military upon graduation.

Your student can graduate as a commissioned or noncommissioned cadet. If they go the commissioned route, they can enter the military as a second lieutenant. A noncommissioned route means when your student graduates, they could go their merry way with all the leadership training the military provides and become an in-demand professional as a result of that training and discipline.

The Corps of Cadets is a full-on experience, requiring your student to wake up every day for formation and exercise, while ROTC might only require two days per week of this type of military training. Students in both programs have regular academic commitments as well. While your student will have many classes with their fellow Corps of Cadets or ROTC peers, they will also have many classes with traditional, nonmilitary college students.

CORPS OF CADETS

The Corps of Cadets program is only offered at six colleges:
- The Citadel (https://www.citadel.edu/), Charleston, South Carolina
- Norwich University (https://www.norwich.edu/cadets), Northfield, Vermont
- Texas A&M University (https://corps.tamu.edu/), College Station, Texas
- University of North Georgia, Dahlonega, Georgia
- Virginia Military Institute (https://ung.edu/military-college-admissions/the-military-college-of-georgia.php), Lexington, Virginia
- Virginia Tech (https://vtcc.vt.edu/), Blacksburg, Virginia

These colleges bear the federal designation of senior military colleges.

The Corps of Cadets program comes in different shapes and sizes. For example, at Virginia Military Institute, the entire student body is made up of cadets, while other programs, like Texas A&M University, have a mix of traditional students and cadets. The Corps of Cadets is just a subset of the larger student population.

Texas A&M has one of the oldest and largest programs in the country, dating back to 1876. Until recently, the program only offered partial scholarships to anyone joining the program. The corps started at Texas A&M when the university, under a different name, was an all-male school. Students were required to be part of the Cadet Corps until the college became coed in 1964. Texas A&M has continued to produce a significant number of commissioned officers throughout the years.

As an incoming cadet, your student can receive partial to full scholarships based on their personal circumstances and each program. At Texas A&M, for example, incoming and current cadets are eligible for Cadet Corps scholarships between $1,000 and $10,000. Some of the factors considered in awarding these scholarships are grades, leadership, community involvement, and financial need. Cadets might also be eligible for other scholarships.

ROTC

ROTC is a program that runs concurrently with your student's regular college program, and it is offered at more than 1,700 colleges and universities. It offers full and partial merit-based scholarships. Your student can join the ROTC program at various points in their college career. However, many students apply to join before they enter college. Depending on when your student joins the program and other factors, they can get up to 100 percent tuition coverage. By going through this program, it's possible to join the military as an officer.

Merit scholarships are available and, at the time of this writing, can be as high as $100,000. In addition, students receive annual allowances for books along with a monthly stipend.

If they're interested in joining the ROTC program, your student doesn't need to receive a scholarship. However, if they get a scholarship, they must serve in the Army for four years. If they enroll in the ROTC Advanced Course, they must complete a three-year service period.

TYPES OF ROTC PROGRAMS

The Navy, Army, and Air Force have ROTC programs. Most officers come to the military by way of the ROTC. Students interested in joining the Marines go through the Navy ROTC program, and those interested in serving in the Space Force (https://www.spaceforce.mil/About-Us/About-Space-Force/) would have to go through the Air Force ROTC program.

────────── *The Air Force ROTC Program* ──────────

This program is offered at 1,100 colleges in the United States, and your student must commit to serve four years of active duty in the Air Force or Space Force upon completion of the program. If in aviation, they might have to serve longer.

Program benefits and requirements:
- Academic standards
- Fitness requirements
- Medical requirements
- Guaranteed career as an officer in the Air Force or Space Force

For more information, visit US Air Force ROTC (https://www.afrotc.com/what-it-takes/).

The Army ROTC Program

This program is offered at more than one thousand colleges in the United States. Upon completion of the program, your student will be able to work as a second lieutenant in the Army or Army Reserve of the Army National Guard.

Program benefits and requirements:
- 100 percent tuition coverage and funds to cover books and costs of living
- Training within the college curriculum
- Leadership skill development
- Guaranteed career as an Army officer

For more information, visit: US Army ROTC (https://www.goarmy.com/careers-and-jobs/find-your-path/army-officers/rotc.html).

CHAPTER 10: Strategy #8: Consider the Military

The Navy and Marine Corps ROTC Program

The Navy ROTC program is very similar to the Air Force and Army in that it is run alongside your student's regular college program. If they join this program, they must complete their regular course work requirements toward their degree, plus take classes in Naval Science and other subjects. They are also expected to participate in physical training. Leadership is a major focus of these programs.

The Navy ROTC also has a preparatory program with a focus on closing the achievement gap between students from under-resourced backgrounds and their peers. These are one-year programs that prepare students for the academic rigors and life skills required to succeed in the four-year Naval ROTC programs.

At the end of the four-year programs, graduates of the program are guaranteed a position in the Navy or Marine Corps as an officer.

Program benefits include:
- Scholarships
- Leadership training and experience
- Guaranteed careers

For more information, visit: US Navy ROTC (https://www.netc.navy.mil/Commands/Naval-Service-Training-Command/NROTC/Program-Info/#NSB).

ARE MILITARY ACADEMIES OR ROTC PROGRAMS RIGHT FOR YOUR STUDENT?

The requirements and process to get into an ROTC or Cadet Corps program look very different than that of a military academy program. In assessing these programs, it's important to look past the financial benefit to determine if it's a good fit.

First, there are the academic requirements.

Second, your student must be physically up to the task. Not only are they required to take a physical assessment to get into most of these programs, but they must also maintain a certain body mass or run the risk of losing their scholarship.

Third, your student must consider whether the highly structured and disciplined style of the military programs is one they could easily adjust to.

Beyond helping your student reduce their college debt, these programs can help them develop a strong sense of purpose and unmatched leadership skills. Students going through these programs will find themselves in demand after college because employers tend to see them as more mature than their peers.

Students often find camaraderie and develop great friendships in these programs. If your child is not already very disciplined in time-management, they will have no choice but to get there and survive. The ROTC and Corps of Cadets can be great alternatives to entering an academy.

CHAPTER 10: Strategy #8: Consider the Military

To learn more about these programs:
1. Attend information sessions. If you and your student can attend these sessions, you can talk to someone who attended one of these institutions. This way, you and your student will get a firsthand account of what it's like.
2. Have your student talk to their high school counselor. More than likely, their counselor has worked with students who have joined the academies and will be able to provide adequate guidance.
3. Visit the campus. Whether it's West Point in New York or the Air Force Academy in Colorado Springs, you and your student will get to see a day in the life of a cadet and observe some of the rich traditions. In addition, these campuses and surrounding cities are quite beautiful.

These military options can be a great way to help pay for college and gain valuable skills and experience. Not only will they provide your student with financial assistance, but they will also teach them the values of discipline, teamwork, and leadership that will help them in any career. If they're considering enrolling in one of these programs, do your research and discuss it together to understand what they're signing up for. If this is the path they choose to take, they can obtain a well-rounded education without getting into too much debt.

KEY TAKEAWAYS

If you think a military option is a good fit or to learn more about them, your student could do the following:
1. Talk to their high school counselor.
2. Start preparing before junior year of high school if they are planning to apply to the academies; there are many steps in the process.
3. Attend an Academy Nomination Information Session usually hosted by your congressional representative. These events often have academy representatives there to answer questions too. Check your representative's website for details or call their office.
4. Explore the military academies.
    - US Military Academy (https://www.westpoint.edu/)
    - US Naval Academy (https://www.usna.edu/homepage.php)
    - US Coast Guard Academy (https://uscga.edu/)

- US Merchant Marine Academy (https://www.usmma.edu/)
- US Air Force Academy (https://www.usafa.af.mil/)

5. Explore ROTC programs.
   - Army ROTC
   - Navy ROTC
   - Navy ROTC Marine Option
   - Air Force ROTC

6. Explore the Corps of Cadets programs.
   - The Citadel (https://www.citadel.edu/), Charleston, South Carolina
   - Norwich University (https://www.norwich.edu/cadets), Northfield, Vermont
   - Texas A&M University (https://corps.tamu.edu/), College Station, Texas
   - University of North Georgia, Dahlonega, Georgia
   - Virginia Military Institute (https://ung.edu/military-college-admissions/the-military-college-of-georgia.php), Lexington, Virginia
   - Virginia Tech (https://vtcc.vt.edu/), Blacksburg, Virginia

Conclusion

It is clear that reducing student debt is a major challenge facing many families as they prepare their children for college. According to a 2023 article by Hahn and Tarver in *Forbes*, Americans now owe $1.75 trillion in student debt.[2] Yet, with thoughtful planning and hard work, you can minimize the student debt you and your child take on.

This book has outlined various strategies families can use to reduce college expenses, from exploring scholarship opportunities to taking advantage of early collegiate high schools and community colleges. I sincerely hope that by utilizing these methods, you can lessen the overall financial burden that college can bring. With ample research and planning, you can ensure your child will get the education they need to succeed without compromising their financial future.

The first step in this process is to understand how financial aid works. To access most financial aid, you'll have to complete the FAFSA. Financial aid comes from grants, scholarships, loans, and work-study. Grants and scholarships don't typically need to be repaid and are given based on the student's academic achievement or financial need. Loans must be repaid, usually with interest, and come from government or private lenders. Work-study is a form of federal aid that will allow you to earn money in exchange for work. By the way, colleges generally add loans to financial aid packages your child might receive if accepted. However, just because loans are offered to you, it doesn't mean you have to take them. Make a budget and stick to it.

College access programs, early college high schools, and the military are excellent options to reduce your college bill by 50 to 100 percent. Some of the top national college access programs, Posse and QuestBridge, can get your child into very selective colleges on a full scholarship.

It is also essential to research different types of scholarships, their eligibility requirements, and steps for obtaining them. Some will come directly from colleges; others, considered private scholarships, will come from foundations and other organizations. Many private scholarships are available, so feel free to—or have your child—do a deep dive into a scholarship database like thecollegepod.com. You can contact your child's high school counseling office for the most up-to-date local scholarship information. They will generally have a list of what other students have won, and they are usually the main point of contact for organizations like Rotary when advertising scholarships in schools. In addition, you can google the name of your city plus "foundation" to find out about scholarships awarded by foundations in most cities.

Last, if your child is considering joining the military via the academies or ROTC, speak to a military representative or your state's congressional representative to get information about your student's military options.

With all the resources available and the strategies mentioned in this book, you'll give your child the freedom to explore higher education, and life in general, without financial worry.

Remember, while you want to give your child the best possible education, you will be able to manage your overall costs if you only pursue the colleges you can afford. Try using the net price calculator (see end of Chapter 3) to get an early estimate of how much gift aid your child might receive from a particular college. And don't dismiss a college because it's private or their published price looks too high. In some cases, after scholarships and grants, a private college with a high sticker price can cost less than your state university.

In many cases, a student's success will not be determined by which college they attend, but instead by the major they pursue and what they do with the opportunities available (e.g., internships, mentors, network). According to an analysis of several studies on the value of a degree published in *The Economist*, "What you study generally matters more than where you do it."[24] For example, a student who pursues a STEM major will generally be able to break into a high-paying career, regardless of whether they attend Duke or University of Kansas.

If you apply one or more of the strategies outlined in this book, you can avoid the mistakes many parents make. And you can wave goodbye to sending your child to a college you can't afford. Good luck!

REFERENCES

1. Kerr E, Wood S. See How Average Student Loan Debt Has Changed. U.S. News & World Report. September 13, 2022. Accessed September 4, 2023. https://www.usnews.com/education/best-colleges/paying-for-college/articles/see-how-student-loan-borrowing-has-changed
2. Hahn, A. & Tarver, J. Student Loan Debt Statistics: Average Student Debt. Forbes. 2023. Accessed May 2, 2023. https://www.forbes.com/advisor/student-loans/average-student-loan-statistics/
3. Carnevale, A., Rose, S., & Cheah B. (n.d.). The College Payoff. Georgetown University Center on the Education and the Workforce. Accessed January 5, 2023. https://cew.georgetown.edu/cew-reports/the-college-payoff/
4. Hanson, M. Average Cost of College and Tuition. Education Data Initiative. 2023. Accessed April 30, 2023. https://educationdata.org/average-cost-of-college#:~:text=The%20average%20cost%20of%20attendance,or%20%24218%2C004%20over%204%20years
5. Urban Institute. Student Loan Debt and Access to Homeownership for Borrowers. November 2022. Accessed April 30, 2023. https://www.urban.org/sites/default/files/2022-11/Student%20Loan%20Debt%20and%20Access%20to%20Homeownership%20for%20Borrowers%20of%20Color.pdf
6. College Board. Trends in College Pricing and Student Aid 2022. 2022. Accessed August 30, 2022. https://research.collegeboard.org/media/pdf/trends-in-college-pricing-student-aid-2022.pdf
7. Hanson, M. Average Cost of College Textbooks. Education Data Initiative. 2022. Accessed April 30, 2023. https://educationdata.org/average-cost-of-college-textbooks.
8. Morrison N. Black graduates twice as likely to be unemployed. Forbes. June 18, 2020. Accessed April 10, 2023. https://www.forbes.com/sites/nickmorrison/2020/06/18/black-graduates-twice-as-likely-to-be-unemployed/?sh=2acca7fc77eb.
9. Zapp, Daniel. 2019 Money Matters on Campus. EVERFI. AIG Retirement Services. Accessed February 10, 2022: https://everfi.com/white-papers/financial-education/2019-money-matters-report/
10. Adedoyin, O. As More Stressed-Out Students Consider Dropping Out, Surgeon General Pushes College Leaders to Ramp Up Support. The Chronicle of Higher Education. August 30, 2022. Accessed April 30, 2023. https://www.chronicle.com/article/as-stressed-out-students-consider-dropping-out-u-s-surgeon-general-pushes-college-leaders-to-ramp-up-support
11. Terry Long, Bridget. Is College Worth It? Yes, But Not Always. Payscale. Accessed August 30, 2022. https://www.payscale.com/content/value-college-degree.pdf
12. White House. President Biden Announces Student Loan Relief for Borrowers who need it most. August 24, 2022. Accessed January

5, 2023. https://www.whitehouse.gov/briefing-room/statements-releases/2022/08/24/fact-sheet-president-biden-announces-student-loan-relief-for-borrowers-who-need-it-most/?utm_source=link

13 National Association of College and University Business Officers. Tuition Discount Rates at Private Colleges and Universities Top 50 Percent. Accessed April 30, 2023. https://www.nacubo.org/Press-Releases/2023/Tuition-Discount-Rates-at-Private-Colleges-and-Universities-Top-50-Percent

14 Sallie Mae. How America Pays for College. Accessed May 2, 2023. https://www.salliemae.com/about/leading-research/how-america-pays-for-college/

15 Levine, P, Desjean, J. The Complication with the FAFSA Simplification. Brookings Institute. April 17, 2023. Accessed April 30, 2023. https://www.brookings.edu/research/the-complication-with-fafsa-simplification/

16 Community College Research Center. Community College FAQs. Accessed September 1, 2023. https://ccrc.tc.columbia.edu/community-college-faqs.html

17 US News. Early College Programs: What to Know. November 11, 2022. Accessed May 2, 2023. https://www.usnews.com/education/best-high-schools/articles/early-college-programs-what-to-know#:~:text=There%20are%20about%20400%20early,making%20these%20programs%20relatively%20rare

18 Community College Research Center. Community College FAQs. Accessed September 1, 2023. https://ccrc.tc.columbia.edu/community-college-faqs.html

19 U.S. Bureau of Labor Statistics. Occupational Outlook Handbook. (n.d.). Accessed September 1, 2023. https://www.bls.gov/ooh/

20 Fusaro, M. College Remediation: Who Needs It, and Does It Help? Harvard Graduate School of Education. July 18, 2007. Accessed April 17, 2023. https://www.gse.harvard.edu/ideas/usable-knowledge/07/07/college-remediation-who-needs-it-and-does-it-help

21 Center for American Progress. Strengthening our Economy through College for All. Accessed April 30, 2023. https://www.americanprogress.org/article/strengthening-our-economy-through-college-for-all/

22 Campaign for Free College Tuition. Making Public Colleges Tuition Free. Accessed April 30, 2023. https://www.freecollegenow.org/

23 White House. Steps For the Service Academies Application Process. Accessed September 4, 2023. https://www.whitehouse.gov/service-academy-nominations/steps/

24 The Economist. Was Your Degree Really Worth It. April 3, 2023. Accessed July 5, 2023. https://www.economist.com/international/2023/04/03/was-your-degree-really-worth-it